CUBA
IN SPLINTERS

ELEVEN STORIES FROM THE NEW CUBA

Selected and Edited by
ORLANDO LUIS PARDO LAZO

Translated by
HILLARY GULLEY

OR Books
New York · London

Selection © 2014 Orlando Luis Pardo Lazo
Individual stories © 2014 the authors
English translation © 2014 Hillary Gulley
For all rights information: rights@orbooks.com

Published by OR Books, New York and London
Visit our website at www.orbooks.com

First printing 2014

All rights reserved. No part of this book may be reproduced or transmitted in any form or by any means, electronic or mechanical, including photocopy, recording, or any information storage retrieval system, without permission in writing from the publisher, except brief passages for review purposes.

Cataloging-in-Publication data is available from the Library of Congress.
A catalog record for this book is available from the British Library.

ISBN 978-1-939293-48-0 paperback
ISBN 978-1-939293-49-7 e-book

Text design by Bathcat Ltd. Typeset by Lapiz Digital, Chennai, India. Printed by BookMobile in the United States and CPI Books Ltd in the United Kingdom. The U.S. printed edition of this book comes on Forest Stewardship Council-certified, 30% recycled paper. The printer, BookMobile, is 100% wind-powered.

CONTENTS

7 *Preface*
Orlando Luis Pardo Lazo

15 *Fefita and the Berlin Wall*
Jorge Alberto Aguiar Díaz

25 *Epilogue with Superhero and Fidel*
Jorge Enrique Lage

41 *Exorcism Zone*
Jhortensia Espineta

49 *Cuba in Splinters*
Ahmel Echevarría Peré

73 *Havana Light*
Lien Carrazana Lau

85 *Skhizein (Decalogue for the Year Zero)*
Polina Martínez Shviétsova

101 *Third Eye of the Madman*
Michel Encinosa Fú

119 *Thirty Seconds of Western Silence*
Lia Villares

133 *That Zombie Belongs to Fidel!*
Erick J. Mota

151 *Dancing Days*
Raúl Flores

167 *The Man, the Wolf and the New Woods*
Orlando Luis Pardo Lazo

189 *Author Biographies*

PREFACE

In the beginning there was the Revolution and the Revolution was Fidel

The year 2000 didn't mean the advent of a new century and millennium in Cuba. On the contrary, it meant the continuance of a paleo-historical process called The Revolution, capital T, capital R. In neon lights, with regard to the international academy. Perversely polarized and pop. With fireworks and firearms. Utopia embodied in a people despite its people. The same Revolution which, since long before its victory on January 1, 1959, confused part with whole and violently occupied every space in society, including its language, erecting a monolithic model, at the top of which still stands Fidel.

Fidel, no last name required. Sometimes euphonic, sometimes fossil, with its intimate and intimidating F. Perversely as elite as it is populist. Omniscient, ubiquitous, all-encompassing Fidel, the Ultimate Narrator of this totalitarian utopia that he has molded to his image and likeness. The Revolution, understood as a national narrative that distances us from the rest of the planet—the Doppler Defect. What has caused us Cubans to be less contemporary: strange vermin forsaken by God and capital. An experimental paradise for anthropological entomology. The Revolution, with its forced, even-handed alacrity, an ideological idyll which, in the twenty-first century, has yet to expire. Expirevolution. During a period that has already lost its own plot.

CUBA IN SPLINTERS

Wenn ich Kultur höre, entsichere ich meinen Browning

The literature of the Revolution always lacked imagination. I don't know if this was ever attributed to the economic, financial and commercial embargo imposed on our country by the United States—also privately known as the imperialist blockade. Literary rhetoric was therefore forced to adhere to a generic realism: a rosy realism, at times Russian. If literature was to be a "weapon of the Revolution," then it had to be something that could be armed and disarmed by our most humble workers and farmers. In fact, Cuban literature was assigned the special mission of ceasing to be a spiritual luxury and humbly setting forth to create a literate populace. To be understood by everyone, especially the experts in the political police. This is why the "original sin" of our intellectuals, as an ex-social class, is that of never having been "authentically revolutionary," according to the gospel of Ernesto Ché Guevara.

This sin must be radically atoned for, and the sooner the better. In the summer of 1961, Fidel stood at the National Library before hundreds of seated intellectuals, laid his fifteen-shot Browning on a desk and proclaimed: "Within the Revolution, everything. Against the Revolution, nothing," allowing only for a residual "outside" freedom for those who didn't agree with him. With Him. It was clear that in a revolution like the Cuban one, literature was too serious a matter to be left to the men and women of letters.

Within literature, everything. Outside literature, nothing.

In the early 1990s, the fall of the Soviet Union and the European socialist countries put Cuba on the verge of famine and government concentration camps—the so-called Option Zero of the Special Period of War in Times of Peace. This debacle, however, also brought down the Sugar Curtain; Cuban artists felt the stirrings of liberation. The disassembling of centralized control mechanisms meant that, for the first time since 1959, writers could publish their work abroad without permission from the State. For the first time since 1959, the same State allowed writers to collect royalties without clearing bureaucratic hurdles and obtaining a surreal "trust certificate." So literature assumed the role the imprisoned press could not, and anthologies of very critical writers were soon published, like that of the Novísimos generation: *The Last Shall Be the First* (Editorial Letras Cubanas, 1993), compiled by Salvador Redonet. Pandora's box was about to open.

The *Paideia* project, the *La Azotea de Reina* gatherings, the magazine *Diáspora(s)*, among many other independent works, burst forth with an energy suppressed during decades of censorship. It was too much: the official reaction involved paramilitary forces from the political police. It was still unthinkable that there could be a literature independent of State Security, its agents being the specialized readers they were. Most of the main writers of this *perestroikuba* were coerced, blackmailed, fired, marginalized, beaten, jailed and obliged to choose between silence or exile. It was an exceptional victory for the cultural policy of the Communist Party (still the only legal political party in our country). In fact, at the beginning of the 2000s, the insular silence was fathomless. Almost none of those artists stayed in Cuba; they fled to fade away abroad, graciously. In the end, there was silence *and* exile. The change of century and millennium in Cuba didn't bring the 2000s, but the '0s. We had to start from zero.

Y2K

Generations don't exist. Generational illusion does. Generation Year Zero, therefore, can be no more than a band of outlaws, of electrons out of orbit, miracles of the marginal view, the residue of writers who didn't belong to the world of writers but to those of the sciences or the streets, and who therefore conducted themselves like squatters. Generation Year Zero is like an album of rare species in danger of extinction, having met in a single city at the same time the date changed from 1990-something to 2000-nothing. a city starting with H, silent but still so *h*eloquent, a consonant that's useless for Spanish poetry but that couldn't be better-suited for new narrative.

This city, of course, is still called Havana. And this generation, in trying to write its own Genesis 0:0, didn't aspire to be the first, but the last. XYZ: Xeneration Year Zero. To recount drop by drop. To narrate with aphasia and in*fidel*ity. To poke around in the black holes denied by dismemory and invent its own tradition. Discubanocracy. To risk their lives, even, to recount the one thousand, nine hundred and fifty-nine nights of a post-homeland nightmare, clinical and cynical symptom of an entire vo*cuba*lary with which to dynamize and dynamite "Cuban literature" (an oxymoron in quotes).

Words of pixels

The years zero in a Cuba not connected to the Internet were, paradoxically, the Golden Decade of digital magazines. First there was the nearly clandestine boom of independent e-zines, like *Cacharros(s), 33 y un Tercio, DesLiz, La Caja de la China* and *The Revolution Post*, among others. Nearly all of the eleven authors in this anthology first became known by editing and self-publishing in these underground magazines. A phenomenon that was eminently urban, Havanan and amateur, but with the airs of inhabiting a First World megalopolis: delocalization as a strategy for expressive freedom. An alphabet of bits against analogic barbarism and the *ancien régime* of censorship on paper.

There was an urgency in the writing that prioritized narrative over poetry, and that reduced the essay to almost nothing. Following a twentieth century of megalomaniacal monologues from disciplinary powers, we, in our literary discussions, preferred to avoid any counter-theories. The official uniformed Duty had to be opposed with the Pleasure of multiplicities. The historical and homogenous mass had to be confronted with atomized chaos. Only in this Brownian movement could the hope survive of escaping the static sterility of the state. *Libera*ture: a Brownian flight of heretics to survive the Browning belonging to a commander who would never become a cadaver. *Rev in Peace*.

Index & anti-index

This anthology is doubly minimal:

1. Because it does not include all of the writers of this Cuban counter-vanguard. There are many other conceivable 0:0 anthologies, including, for example, Lizabel Mónica, Osdany Morales, Jamila Medina, Ainsley Negrín, Abel Fernández-Larrea, Arnaldo Muñoz Viquillón, Legna Rodríguez, Evelyn Pérez, Carlos Esquivel and Agnieska Hernández (in the summer of 2013, I compiled the writing of some of these authors for *Sampsonia Way Magazine* of City of Asylum/Pittsburgh). These ten absences also belong to the margin of the national mainstream and dialogue polyphonically with the eleven

presences included here: Jorge Alberto Aguiar Díaz, Jorge Enrique Lage, Jhortensia Espineta, Ahmel Echevarría Peré, Lien Carrazana Lau, Polina Martínez Shviétsova, Michel Encinosa Fú, Lia Villares, Erick J. Mota, Raúl Flores and myself. We are twenty-one dissident ghosts who roam and eat away, like cannibals, at the Cuban Caribbean of a twenty-first century that is just getting started. The local color still oversaturates everything, not only because of the island's institutional inertia, but perhaps because the foreign market only asks for more and more of this same Cuban bubble that grows and grows without ever bursting: typical topics, common characters, stereotypical settings and more than familiar forms. In the face of such mediocrity on the part of the media we don't need a good author: we need daring narrators who can be as uncomfortable as needles on end and awaken good readers to what they've been missing.

2. To produce a maximum intensity impact. Against totalitarianism's somber sequel, the sudden slap of a tweet. Cuba in 140 characters or less.

Havana, AC (After Castro)

It is possible that this anthology is the portrait of a family that never was. The communicating vessels between these eleven stories are not bridges, but short-circuits: affinities, violence, tensions between text and anti-text which, coinciding in the same book, produce a collision that consumes its own meaning, generating light. A radiating, incandescent zero of patria-plasma.

From the Berlin Wall to the wall of the Florida Strait. From Fidelozoic-era bodyguards to sex for sale at a regional train station.

Snob Buddhism and sub-socialist zombies, Cuba in splinters of a turbulent insanity that traverses everything: like an ethical axis, kinetic. Fractal stories, allegorical anecdotes that are the continuation of others written by others without clarifying who is who and which is which: plagiarism or provocation? Smoke or pills so the mind can emigrate before the body, beyond the claustrophobic line of the horizon while still inside the claustrophilic skin of an uncivilized citizenship. Hiroshimavana, *mon amour*, the cenotaph city. Remake and collage, coda and epitaph for a *cadavre exquis* who will drink of the wine to come as the future fast forward begins to rewind. No one knows what past awaits us. Antepenultimate visions of the holo*castro*. This anthology couldn't be anything but the portrait of this family that will always be a would-have-been. The future is today. Let it read.

—Orlando Luis Pardo Lazo
Pittsburghavana
January 2014

Fefita and the Berlin Wall
JORGE ALBERTO AGUIAR DÍAZ

Back then I was seeing Fefita, a fifty-year-old black woman with saggy tits and an armored ass. I was JAAD, the visitor, dragging my feet, ideas, and all the paper with the scribbles of my porn novel.

Fefita would always wait for me on the patio, and we were happy together. After we'd finish screwing, I would talk to her about literature. She had never read a book in her life. They all seemed so boring, she said, too fine and fake.

Fefita would put the coffee on and make lunch. I'd sit there and watch her ass bounce to the beat of my words about words.

I'd fill her head with characters, plot twists, and JAAD's adventures, which always sounded sad and unlikely, even if they were true.

Fefita would crack up at my nasty tales about Bukowski, Lino Novás Calvo, Henry Miller, and Pedro Juan Gutiérrez, a journalist who in those days had tried to write a few piss-poor stories, and showed up at my house one day so I could fix them.

For a while I helped her run a black-market toothpaste operation. One of the neighborhood guys would swipe the stuff from the factory and she would peddle it down at the train station. That's how we'd score a few pesos.

We all accepted that we had to steal. Steal to eat. The government had transformed us into a gang of criminals, and we thought we were heroes if we had four pesos in our pockets. We'd sell discount perfume, powdered milk, cans of Russian meat and anything else that came our way.

Every now and then I'd pump Fefita's ass full of my milk. I like to see my milk all over just about any woman's big fat ass. But if she's black it's even better. She loved it too, so much she'd beg for it. Over and over. Until I'd dry up, and then she'd say:

"You relax, *papito*. I'll go fix you a little steak."

Then half an hour later she'd want my long hard bone again. You bet I was hung long and hard. And I had strength to boot. And I moved like an American blender. Then the years started to catch up with me. My prick shriveled up and started to hang like a dish rag. Now I can hardly move.

But that's another story. Back then I was poor and happy. And there was Fefita with her tight black ass. Sucking my cock like you wouldn't believe.

"Put it here, *papi*, in my little mouth. Give your old woman her bottle. Spoil me, *papi*."

People had to put up with our scandals day and night.

"Can it, perverts!"

"Cradle robber! Have some pride, old hag!"

"How can you like those dirty little white boys, Fefita? Old swine!"

I had just turned twenty-four and ran as ragged as they came. Holes in my shoes. Old clothes. Lice. I worked nights as a custodian and days washing floors in a building on Calle Reina. As the weeks passed I got skinny carrying around that big portfolio where I kept my porn manuscript.

"Let people talk, *papito*. You're going to be a famous writer one day. You're going to have all kinds of women and I'm going to be your love and we're going to have so much fun with all your little white girls."

"That's right, Fefita. We'll find a delicious white girl and live the three of us together. We'll make it out of this dump."

Fefita's room was a hovel. Holes in the walls, light through the cracks in the ceiling, a brightly-lit kitchen and no bathroom. We pissed and shat in a plastic tub.

When we wanted to wash ourselves, we had to use a filthy shared room, which we usually had to wait for out on the patio.

Fefita had lost her eighteen-year-old son to the sea. Every once in a while she'd show me her only picture of him. His father left in

1980, the same year as the Mariel boatlift, "and the son of a bitch never even bothered to write." Fefita would think back and cry.

I'd often show up when she wasn't expecting me. She'd be slumped on her half-rotten bench, sweating from the heat and weepy, having lost the will to cook or live.

"It was a crazy thing to do. But it was right," she would say, staring at the picture. "There's no future for young people in this country."

"There's not even a country, Fefita. We're a mistake."

We'd go out for a walk around the neighborhood. I'd try to cheer her up.

"Come on girl, you just have to keep on living. Remember what Virgilio Piñera said: *They may be killing me but I'm still having fun.*"

She would laugh. She'd flash me her big old tits. And she'd move her big old ass. Then she'd say if she ever met the pansy who said that, it would be the end of his queering around.

And sometimes she'd go out with me. And other times I couldn't even drag her to the corner. She'd curl up on our mattress, which was filthy with fluids and misery, and wait for death.

"That's no way to be, sweetie."

"We're already dead, *papito*, and we have to keep waiting for death to come."

The people out on the patio would fight. They'd listen to music. They'd play dominoes, talk about baseball. And there we were, just Fefita and me, at the end of the universe, naked and spent.

Whenever we emerged from her little dump, everyone would stare. All the white guys would spit and the black guys would look at me askance. The women would sing some dumb song, mutter some double entendre. But Fefita and I would just keep strutting down Gloria, Corrales, Apodaca, all the way to Egido, kissing and petting like newlyweds. That's how we liked to lighten things up.

"Let's go down to the port, *papito*."

She liked the smell of petroleum. We watched the boats. I told her to close her eyes and imagine a bay full of seagulls. I stopped at the sea wall and opened my arms and shouted:

"If I hadn't thought the water was encroaching like a cancer
I could have surrendered peacefully to sleep.
I have grown used to the stink of the port,
Country of mine, so young and not yet defined!
Eternal misery is the act of remembrance,
Town of mine, so young and not organized!
Life in the basin with the scum of rage,
No one can leave! No one can leave!
Light kills a village just like the plague,
And what good is the sun in such a sad place?"

She got all nervous and told me to shut up.

"For your mother's sake, *papito*, here comes a cop."

And then she remembered what I had said about Virgilio Piñera. She began to fuss and flutter.

"I'm scared. I'm so scared," she said.

The cop looked us up and down as if we were a pair of lunatics and crossed the street. And we were a pair of lunatics.

When we didn't have the money for rum we'd make some sugar water and go down to the station. We'd find a spot where we could sit and watch the trains. We looked like a couple of kids watching those locomotives whistle. The station cafeteria sold stale, fly-covered bread with pasta for one peseta. And that's what we'd eat. Then she'd talk about El Verraco, the little town in Santiago de Cuba where she was born.

"One of these days I'm going to get on one of those trains and go. Havana's nothing but a big loony bin now."

And it was. Havana was flooded with lunatics and beggars, prostitutes and policemen. When we heard the news that communism had fallen in the Soviet Union, everyone poured into the streets to wait.

Then the little food we had disappeared. Everyone was famished. We were walking cadavers, our faces contorted into grimaces of death. And horror. Groups of two or three undercover cops appeared on every corner in case anyone started to mouth off about the government.

Fefita and I would wake up hopeful and go to bed even more hopeful.

"It's going to fall here any day now, Fefita."

And we'd fuck on empty stomachs. Then one day even the bread with pasta disappeared from the station. People with money had nothing left to buy. Most of the time we'd just eat rice. Fefita would save the leftovers and we'd eat them for breakfast the next morning with water. Sugar was a luxury.

"It doesn't matter, Fefita. It's going to fall any day now. Then you can go off to your town and I'll write whatever I can milk out of my dick."

Fidel appeared on TV. Stern, haggard, he had aged in just a few weeks: "We'll sink the island first. Socialism or death," he said, closing his speech.

He looked desperate, and I had the feeling these hours would be his last in power.

I got the news through my father. He had a short-wave radio and we would listen to Radio Martí. The communist countries fell one by one. When Czechoslovakia fell I thought of Milan Kundera. Fefita thought of her son.

"See? He goes and drowns and now look. This guy is going to fall and I don't even have my son."

And the days went. And our hope went. And I didn't write one more line of my porn novel.

One weekend I didn't go over to Fefita's place. I was sick. I didn't even have the strength to walk to Jesús María. Three days in bed drinking soup that was just hot water and listening to the news. Sick in body and mind. Sick with history. Sick with fear.

People were waiting for something big to happen, they began to speak of freedom. And we didn't know when the town would fill the streets and come undone like wild beasts. They had trained us to be obedient dogs with our tails between our legs. But we were rabid dogs who had been abandoned by our master.

I woke up on Monday feeling better. I walked over to Fefita's and ran into a *mulato* who lived around there.

"Hey white boy, where the fuck do you live?" he asked.

"What's your problem, bro? What do you care?"

"Don't play tough, white boy. I'm asking because Fefita left us, and nobody knew where you lived to go and tell you."

"What do you mean Fefita left...?"

"Yeah, *compadre*. She's gone. Heart attack."

I went to her room. It had been taped off by the Urban Reform Office. Her neighbors told me everything. Someone gave me water and coffee. I stayed late hanging around the patio.

She had died Saturday afternoon. They buried her that same day since she didn't have any relatives. She died in bed. An old lady handed me my portfolio of papers and said:

"They found her with this. It looks like she was reading it when she died."

That night I went to the station. The bread with pasta had reappeared, but I wasn't hungry and the line was endless. Three guys got into a brawl and pushed a pregnant lady, who was on the verge of vomiting her fetus.

I sat down to watch the locomotives. Ecstatic. Useless. All the trains had been suspended until further notice.

Everyone kept saying the government was going to fall any minute. When I went to bed, I thought about how Fefita should be alive so we could keep fucking and she could see the end of the story that, at the time, was thirty years old.

Back then, only thirty years old. Now thirty years seems like nothing.

A new slogan began to appear. On the walls, the fences, the building facades, the buses, everywhere: *Thirty-one and onward!* And people just smiled, waiting for the end.

And I wrote, without fear of being ridiculous or repressed, right under one of those many placards: *I love you, Fefita. Ideologies die, love is immortal.*

Time has passed.

I'm still here, hanging around the streets of Havana.

I don't have lice or holes in my shoes. And I don't smell. I'll be an old man soon. I'm no longer poor, or very happy.

All I have to brag about are the beginnings of a bald spot, a toothless mouth and a piece of junk between my legs.

The government is still there. The people are resigned to living without much food or any freedom.

Ten years later, Fefita is a pile of ashes like the Berlin Wall.

I think about Fefita. Fuck, I miss Fefita.

Fefita with her saggy old tits and her armored ass. All of fifty then, and she could be my grandmother now.

I wander through Jesús María, Los Sitios or San Leopoldo. All the neighborhoods look the same. Fefita is a ghost pissing and shitting in a plastic tub.

I think how one day I should go back to writing my porn novel. In the meantime, on the placard that announces the political slogan of the moment, I write: *Our friends leave the country or die.*

My memory is becoming a graveyard.

Epilogue with Superhero and Fidel
JORGE ENRIQUE LAGE

Through the windshield, crumbling suburbs and industrial wasteland. I find some music for the last few miles: hip-hop, Los Aldeanos.

Dirt roads. I drive on, then stop. Pull up near a broken fence. Double-check the sketch someone drew for me, tucked among my torn maps of northern New Jersey. The spot marked with an X. It's here.

From the outside it looks like some kind of warehouse or garage riddled with bullet spray. I look around before going in. A few trees. A garbage heap. The gray horizon. No one for miles around. Inside, the light streaming in from the holes illuminates layers of dust and rust. Cables and chains hang from the ceiling.

"Back here," says a voice.

He's sitting on some old tires. In his hand is the same sketch I had been carrying in my pocket. It's not hard to imagine how he got his hands on it.

"Velazco," I say.

He doesn't blink. He knows his identity has been leaked and is getting around. He lights a match and holds it to the paper.

"I don't know who that is," he replies.

It's my turn to bring up the contacts in Newark and Manhattan, and to make, as a kind of code word, an obscure reference to *El Viaje*, by Miguel Collazo (the comic-book version). Velazco gives me a halfhearted smile and tells me to sit down.

"You wouldn't believe all the types that try to find me. Forget about the shit-eaters at the CIA and the FBI. Some Peruvian from Palm Beach who can shoot lasers from his knuckles. A Salvadorian from Austin who can free the energy contained in matter so it explodes like a nuclear bomb. A boy without papers who wears a phosphorescent suit with butterfly wings and whose powers nobody even knows. Tijuanodon, who is like a dinosaur. Telephonika and Ww-Man (WonderwomanMan), from Virginia. Oh, and there's Captain Idaho . . . They want to form a group. Include me in who knows what. Saving the world, of course, but also some kind of an academic journal called *Hispano Superhero Review*."

Velazco lights a cigarette. "Are you ready?"

I immediately hook up him up to a microphone, adjust the camera, and begin filming.

He is not entirely sure when it all started, when *he* started, but he'd swear it had to do with that absurd accident in the Soviet Union. In Cuba, Velazco had graduated from the Academy of the Ministry of the Interior. He was the product of an elite military education. One day they told him, vaguely, that he had been selected for a special training program in the USSR.

They moved him to a deserted territory somewhere in Central Asia. At first he thought they were sending him to outer space. Those shiny buildings isolated from all civilization were not unlike solitary space stations.

But as time passed there was no indication that the "special program" would become more concrete. No one issued him any orders. Or at least anything that sounded like an order. No one seemed to care that he didn't speak a word of Russian. His comrades, bears from the steppe who seemed less lost than he was, talked amongst themselves in a combination of Barbarian dialects. They communicated with Velazco in gestures and smiles. In this generally lackadaisical atmosphere, hours were spent on card games and bottles of vodka, and the loading and unloading of strange and very volatile equipment. Nobody seemed to know what exactly they were doing there. Until one day something happened.

He was taking a nap down in the labyrinthine basement a few floors underground. What happened? An explosion, maybe, or a leak; someone pulled the wrong lever or pushed the wrong button. Velazco never found out. All he could hear was a loud buzzing and the terrified voices of the steppe tribes as they dashed around, and then nothing. He lost consciousness.

When he came to, he was in a little prop plane headed for Moscow. The pilot, an impenetrable Kazakh man, only knew one phrase in Spanish: *Yo no comprendo*. Velazco didn't either. He left just as he had come: without understanding a thing.

Once he got back to Cuba, his superiors didn't know what to do with him. After some extended vacation time, he was assigned to Personal Security. It was only a matter of time before Velazco managed to stand out. Soon, after he was promoted to Captain, he was appointed as an escort to Fidel Castro. That's when he discovered his power.

"Do you feel something?" I asked him. "Like, when you do it, what is it like?"

"It feels normal," says Velazco. "Like moving your foot or your hand. You move it and that's it. You control it."

"But the first time you did it…"

"It doesn't matter," Velazco blinks, pensive. "What I remember perfectly is the first time I *touched* Fidel. Ah, yes. That was like losing my virginity."

He discovered he could stop time. Time became an extension of him, a part of his body's activity. In the beginning, he stopped time without meaning to. But little by little he learned to control it. As if he were learning to control a muscle, or his breath…

To stop time meant bringing everything—absolutely everything—to a standstill: clocks, people, things moving in the street, a leaf blowing in the wind. Everything except for Velazco himself. Time pressed on for him alone. Velazco had breathing room in this frozen space, and could move freely through it. Reality became a photograph, a snapshot, with Velazco standing just to its side. He could touch things, enter and exit buildings, search people—in short, he could do whatever he wanted. It was like an interval of immunity, and impunity. No one was the wiser once time started back up again, when Velazco decided to press play.

Of course he kept his power a secret. Until one day.

It was the year '90 or '91. The last devastating decade of the Cuban twentieth century had begun. Velazco was on the job. He was standing several feet from Fidel, who was delivering a speech. The speech ended, Fidel backed away from the microphones and took a few steps. Velazco immediately positioned himself to his side. Then he saw, out in the crowd, a few movements that weren't entirely out of the ordinary, but of the sort that awakened his reflexes, his professional instincts. Without even thinking, he brought his hand to Fidel's arm. He held it there an instant. And the applause immediately stopped. The slogan-chanting mouths froze open . . .

Under duress, Velazco had stopped time without meaning to. He quickly restarted it. Then, through the hum of the crowd, he heard a low voice:

"Did you do that?"

Velazco gulped.

"Do what, *Comandante*?"

"Stop time."

"I . . . that is . . ."

A few ministers approached and Velazco stepped away. How could he have noticed? Some kind of supernatural perception? *It was the contact*, Velazco thought bitterly. *I stopped time without meaning to when I was touching the Jefe on his arm. Just my luck.*

Hours later, Fidel summoned him to his office.

"I need an explanation for your little trick, Captain."

Since there wasn't much to explain, Velazco could only insist that he had never used his power for evil. Lately he only stopped time when he was very tired and needed a break to sleep a few hours so he could do his job better. And not only that, but he had never taken another person out of time with him before. The *Comandante* was the only one, and no one else knew a thing. In fact, he didn't even know that when he touched someone . . .

"Let's do it again," Fidel said.

Velazco softly placed his hand on Fidel's arm. They went out to the patio. Fidel looked all around in wonder, like a child.

"And now can you make it go again whenever you want?"

"Yes . . . No . . . Whenever *you* want, *Comandante*."

Fidel stared transfixed at the paralyzed water in the swimming pool.

"It's like a parenthesis in time," he said. "Extra time."

•

Velazco speaks slowly, wearily, with a trace of sadness, and every now and again he takes a long pause and tells me to stop recording.

"You must know that I'm not going to tell you everything."

I tell him now is the time, this is his chance. He nods, convinced. There is a hardness to his face that makes him look older than he really is.

"Think of the future," I insist. "Think of all those young Cubans."

"No. Some of this I'll take to my grave. There are some things a man can never tell. I take all my failures seriously, but also my responsibility. Maybe the young people today don't understand. That's their problem. I couldn't care less."

•

One day Fidel remarked that, in his opinion, the young man whose name he could not recall deserved a promotion. They promoted him immediately.

Major Velazco found himself even closer to Fidel. And he had a secret mission: to stop time for the *Comandante* whenever he ordered it, by way of a signal. He can't remember how many times he did it. During countless official acts, in the middle of countless more speeches. Fidel would take a breather to think or to look for a statistic or simply to contemplate, without having to speak, the multitude of statues amassed before him.

He also requested it in his private life. To sleep outside of time without losing valuable hours that he could spend on reading. To catch something about to slip away on one of his underwater fishing expeditions. For endless pranks and whims that Velazco learned, little by little, to anticipate.

One day Fidel gave him a package. Velazco pulled out an iridescent fabric.

"Your new uniform. Put it on now. I'll turn around if you want."

"That won't be necessary, *Comandante* . . ."

He stripped right then and there and put on the one-piece blue suit with its red belt, a pair of white shoes and a kind of helmet that concealed his eyes and nose. Everything was very tight. The Lycra fabric made his muscles pop. He felt ridiculous. Through his helmet's viewfinder he observed Fidel looking him up and down with satisfaction.

"I had it made myself. In the colors of our flag. You should feel proud, Major."

A small ceremony of two soon followed, at which Fidel presented Velazco with a Superhero medal, designed especially for him, issued by the Republic of Cuba.

"Extraman . . . the Extratime Man. My escort with the extra function . . . Yes, Extraman. From now on you'll answer to that name whenever you are wearing your suit. And you will wear the suit whenever you are on duty."

"That means everyone will see me dressed this way," Extraman wavered.

"Don't you worry about that," Fidel replied. "It looks sharp."

"Pardon me, but won't people think it's a little strange . . . When they see me . . . What will people think, *Comandante*?"

"They won't think anything, they won't even notice you. You'll always be near me. They'll see you, but they won't see you." Fidel rubbed his hands together, smiling. "Remember, I have superpowers too."

He was right, he was always right. From then on, it was as if Fidel had draped a blanket of invisibility over him. Incognito in his new superhero uniform, Velazco/Extraman accompanied the *Comandante* everywhere.

They would cruise around in his Mercedes Benz. Fidel would give the signal, Velazco would take him by the arm, stop time, and Fidel would walk through the streets of Frozen Havana while Velazco followed him at a respectful distance, allowing him space.

The *Comandante* liked these walks. He would stroll through all the people turned to statues, inspect them up close. He would perch on any street corner and observe everything with profound interest, with infinite calm, as if he were in a museum. He would even go in and out of the houses, shops, empty bars and full ones. He would rest for a while, meditate, and then continue walking and nosing around until he became lost.

Velazco would help him find the Mercedes again. Once they arrived, time and the car would continue on their way. They would return to the Counsel of State. In a given day, Fidel might require his services several more times. Velazco stood on guard with only one door between them. Sooner or later, the door would always swing open, and time would again freeze, and then Fidel would go down to the Plaza de la Revolución.

Extraman spent countless hours watching Fidel there in the early morning hours before dawn, alone, in the deserted Plaza, contemplating the untwinkling stars, the satellites halted mid-trajectory, waving his arms for no reason, as if he still did not believe it was possible.

•

"So when did you take off your superhero suit?"

"Before I went home, on my days off. Of course I had very few days off, as you can imagine. I was almost always dressed as Extraman."

Velazco paused and added:

"I ended up getting used to it. One can get used to anything."

"And you never showed the suit to anyone?"

"Well, I was separated from my wife. I lived alone. I didn't speak to the neighbors. I didn't have any friends outside of work and none of them seemed to notice that my uniform had changed. Who was there to show it to if everyone could already see it for themselves?"

And I think, and can't stop thinking, about how many things we had in plain sight that we never really saw. Because we didn't know where or how to look. Because we never bothered to look into the shadows.

And still, little by little, they all come into view. Stories leave a trace, they emerge. The mysterious character (his silhouette, his colors, his extravagant attire) left a subliminal imprint on more than one perturbed retina. A freak rumor began to circulate. Someone went even further: they believed it. And they managed to convince more people. And a fanatic sect soon formed that began to ask questions, examine blown up photographs and put things together. As people made connections the issue grew in secret. If the first objective was to know the truth, the second was to find and record it.

Velazco says:

"I'm sorry, but I don't have much more to tell you."

•

And then the impossible happened. Fidel Castro fell gravely ill and turned over the Government to his brother. The bodyguards were relocated. A few weeks later, they called Velazco in for an interview.

"Sit down, Major Velazco. Or should I say . . . Extraman?"

Raúl Castro informed him that as of that moment he should consider himself dismissed from the Ministry of the Interior. He was placed on leave.

"I don't understand, General."

"Think of it as an early retirement. Without pay."

"What should I do now?"

"That's your problem. You should have thought of that before you started using your superpowers around here. Time is not a toy, Velazco."

. . .

"Fidel shared his suspicions. He said you could be manipulating time, who knows to what ends. He told me you were a danger. And in my experience, Fidel is never wrong."

. . .

"You have nothing to say? Fine, you can leave. Oh, and don't forget to turn in your medal and superhero suit. They no longer belong to you."

Velazco walked toward the door. He turned.

"Could you do me a favor, General? Could you give the *Comandante* a message from me?"

Raúl studied him a few seconds as he drummed his fingers on the table. He nodded.

"Tell him that I hope he gets better soon. And that he is the real superhero."

And Velazco went home, to lead a life that was as normal as possible.

Very soon he began to notice he was under increasing surveillance. They were monitoring his house, all his movements. They were dressed in civilian clothing. They didn't bother to hide. Only by stopping time could Velazco escape the constant surveillance, and feel as if he were the one watching them.

An illusion. He couldn't retreat for the rest of his life into a giant postcard of reality: the price was asphyxiation, the most absolute solitude, as if he were the last survivor of the end of the world.

So he put up with the surveillance, thinking it was a necessary stage, hoping that one day it would taper off and finally cease. But instead it intensified. They would call him on the phone only to apologize, claiming to have the wrong number. (He didn't speak with anyone, so there would be nothing to spy on.) Strangers in the street would make thinly-veiled threats. Velazco grew frightened. There was no way of knowing how far it would go.

One day he stopped time in his house and calmly left for the airport. There he found a direct flight to the United States. He stopped time again just before they closed the doors to the plane. He entered, hid, and started time again for the short flight across the Florida Strait. After he landed, he put the whole operation in reverse so he could disembark.

He was in Miami.

He had simply appeared there. No one saw him leave and no one saw him arrive.

Of course he didn't stay there. He knew too well that the city was infested with spies from both shores, double and even triple agents. All of southern Florida was the same. Even the swamps were teeming with them.

He fled the state. Zigzagged across the Great Plains. He would stop time, appear, then disappear. He used fake names and stories. He never stopped moving around. He always had the feeling they were on his trail. He had all the time in the world. If we found him, it was because he let us.

•

Velazco falls silent. He stubs out his last cigarette.

"We're done," he says, standing up. "Now leave me in peace. I don't want to hear another word about it, ok?"

"That was the agreement... We're very grateful to you."

Unnerved, I take the camera. I gather my things. When I look up, no one is there. I'm alone. Velazco has disappeared.

The question makes no sense, but I still wonder how long I stood there, paralyzed in time like a statue, while he took off for who knows where.

I step out into a New Jersey sunset and walk quickly back to the car. I make a phone call. They're waiting for me at a nearby motel. I put the key in the ignition and for a moment I think: *Will the car explode? Will I go flying through the air in a cloud of fire and dust and charred film?*

I turn the key. Nothing happens. I floor the accelerator. Now the important thing is to not let go of the video.

Exorcism Zone
JHORTENSIA ESPINETA

As if someone had cast a piece of trash from the shadows, a fly appeared under the neon lights, now opaque with time. It dove into the nose of an old man sitting nearby, only to be sent into the air again with a hazard swipe of his hand, finally landing on some dog poop between the rails.

"We have to wait for the train to fill up before we can go, just like with the taxis. Right, Mamá?"

Before the child could lick the ice cream, which was dripping down his fingers, the fly landed on it.

"Mamá, look! The little fly can't fly!"

His mother looked at the fly as it fluttered in the pinkish gelatin, picked it out with her fingers and flicked it onto the platform.

"Hey kiddo, you've dripped all over yourself."

She wiped the boy's fingers with hers as the boy held the cone in his other hand and began to devour it, squeezing his eyes shut as he stuck out his tongue, so he could eat it up it as quickly as possible.

"Chocolate is better."

"Flavors are in your imagination. They don't exist."

The boy, sitting on the duffel bag, watched the fly as it flailed on the cement. He reached for the fly with his other hand, which now emanated an aroma of strawberries. The insect crawled up onto his fingers as fast as it could and began to make its way across them.

"Look, Mamá, it's alive!"

"You and your ideas."

The woman barely looked at him. She lit a cigarette and fixed her eyes on the same spot as before. The man in the gray suit had been standing there for hours, not moving. From time to time he would take out an apparatus into which he spoke, or through which they spoke to him, only turning his head from one side to the other, watching something she couldn't see.

The platform was nearly empty, with only ten or twelve people waiting for the train. Everyone else had grown tired of waiting and left. He knew she was looking at him, and that she kept scanning his shoes. After some time, another man in uniform arrived, and they exchanged salutes and the apparatus. The man approached her.

"Where are you going?"

"Wherever the train goes."

He ran his finger under his nose, looked at her thighs.

"Can I help you with something?"

"You can find me a train."

Still focused on her thighs, he commented on her hair. In reality, it was messy and straight. Her cigarette fell into a ray of light.

"Women who smoke are interesting."

"And they have bad breath."

Him with his finger under his nose again. Her trying to discern whether his shoe had a hole or a bad seam.

"You should go back home. It's late, and the kid must be hungry."

"The kid likes to travel."

She couldn't solve the enigma of his shoe. So far he had managed to keep it hidden.

"Pretty women shouldn't travel alone."

"I'm with my son. And I'm not pretty."

"But you have something..."

"At this time of night all women have something."

"Look, I can take you home."

The woman eyed the crease in his pants. It was delicate, and ran from his upper thigh down to his lower leg, where it faded into the top of his shoes. The fabric wasn't starched, though the man was not old enough to know about starching fabric.

"Show me where the bathroom is."

Without lifting her gaze, she gestured to the boy and pointed to the duffel bag.

"You know what to do."

The boy nodded and, still slurping up the last of ice cream, took a wide straddle over the bag. He placed one foot through each handle and draped the strap over his shoulder. When he looked up, his mother was already walking with the man into the station.

"Watch the door for me."

She closed herself into the stall. She tried to look at his shoe from under the door, but couldn't see a thing. She began to take down her pants, little by little.

"Are you married?" he asked.

"You can't get pregnant just by sucking dicks."

The man looked surprised. There was nothing shameful in the space the woman occupied, though so far he had only looked at her thighs.

"You can have a kid without being married."

"The act of fucking is the same as being married, even if it's only for a second."

The man could hear her urine hitting the toilet thick and hard, as if it were about to shatter the bowl. For him, between those thighs, was a vulva salivating for his tongue, thick lips and a hot, generous vagina with the smell of daytime permeating its walls.

"Come in. A woman doesn't ask a man to accompany her for no reason."

He didn't know what to do. His legs shook. He had never been in a situation like this before. He took a deep breath and entered.

As soon as he was inside, she dove her hand into his fly and pulled out his penis, which looked like a shriveled piece of junk. Its pink head revealed its orifice as if it were a trapped insect. She ran her tongue over it. Then she squeezed her eyes shut and began to violently suck it.

"If you want to come in my mouth it's twenty pesos more."

A block of ice prevented him from speaking. He looked at the woman, who was sitting on the toilet with her pants halfway down, her thighs spilling over the seat, her hair falling into her face.

He began to slowly caress her head as she sank him into her throat.

"If you stroke me . . ."

He wished he had all the money in the world. Without thinking, he lifted his leg—the one he had always managed to hide in the shadows. She saw the shine of his shoe, but with a hole on the inside of the toe. She pulled her head back and, without lifting her eyes from his penis, spat on the floor.

"Don't tell me you don't have any money."

He brought his hand quickly to his pocket.

"I only have fifteen pesos."

She snatched it away from him.

"You can't trust anyone these days. Finish yourself off."

She pulled her pants up the rest of the way outside the stall, with her back turned to him.

"Hey, *señora*, you can't just leave me . . ."

She turned toward him. For the first time he got a good look at her face, and her yellowed eyes filled him with fear.

"You just stiffed me. What else do you want?"

Outside, the boy was still watching the fly, which was showing its last signs of life. She squatted down in front of him and, before kissing him, spat.

"There's no train for us today, either."

Cuba in Splinters
AHMEL ECHEVARRÍA PERÉ

Orlando L. and Henry M. are in the habit of visiting my room. It's as if they plan to arrive at the same time. They appear together, famished, their tongues hanging out like two street dogs. They don't leave until very late. When I have nothing to offer I leave them alone and go out. I never return empty-handed. I can count on Vania and Edith for that.

Henry M. says they are two crafty chicks: "Vania is a cat and Edith is a fox. Everyone wants to bang those two little animals, girls and boys. They'll scratch the hide off anyone who wants to fuck them with one swipe of their paws. They have a very delicate manner of screwing. A sweet way of scratching."

He's right. I had met them at a party. Then I lent them a few books and after three months was afraid I had lost them forever. So I decided to show up at their house, not because I wanted to visit them but more because I wanted my books back. They were expecting me.

I had called them to say I'd be there sometime in the late morning. We hardly noticed the hours passing as we chatted. They invited me to stay for lunch, and to have a few drinks. We drank too much. Once we were drunk we decided to mess around together, and it went badly. Very badly.

Vomit, aspirin, boleros, tears and tangos. The three of us intertwined, naked, enclosed in an apartment. None of us can remember, or care to remember, why we had been crying. Maybe it had been for our friends who had recently left, or because we wanted to cut into that reality.

The exodus had been hacking away at us for over a decade, and it was during that visit when it finally hit us. We wanted to rearrange it, but didn't know how. We bawled our eyes out. We were surrounded by people and alone at the same time. Maybe it was that. Or because we knew the time would come for us to leave too. Or perhaps because we knew the change we wanted would never come from us.

We never spoke of it again, to avoid sounding like shitheads. And though sometimes I still try to imagine how it all would have ended up with Vania and Edith had we not been so depressed, I do know I ended up being best friends with two women who love and look out for each other so much it hurts. We call ourselves the Three Good Soldiers. That's why we go to each other whenever one of us has a problem, and whenever Orlando and Henry come visit, they always clean me out. Vania and Edith's pantry, however, is always full of surprises and at my disposal.

Today Orlando and Henry are at my place. Like always, they're taking up all the space on my bed. They throw themselves onto the plush little bear that sits on my pillow. Yani, my wife, calls it

Teddy, but Orlando, Henry and I secretly call it Honey. A honey-colored bear, soft fur. But Honey is only a nickname, because in reality, for Orlando, its fleece is the memory of Jamy's pubis; for Henry, it's the soft, dense mound of Tania's sex; and for me, well, I just blush whenever Orlando and Henry see me playing with the furry toy.

Yani goes out whenever Orlando and Henry visit. Maybe because we look like a trio of queers. She can't stand our Teddy game. She always tries to take Teddy with her, but Orlando stuffs him under his shirt, throws himself face down and moans: "Don't do it, Yani Yani! Doll of good intentions, don't do it! Look, I'm alone. Very alone. Look how much I miss my Jamy. That slut is so far away. Far. Far. Can't you see my tears? I'm crying. I'm crying and nothing can be done."

Then Henry taunts Orlando: "Who cares if the bitch left. Let her go. She'll be back. And you think twice about crawling back to her. If she does come back, fuck her till her ovaries explode. Shine her thighs, destroy her vagina and yank out her pubes. Then paste them on your chin."

Orlando looks at him sideways, sometimes with hatred, sometimes with envy, and there are days when he has a fist ready to throw and wants nothing more than to spit in his face. Still, the mocking only lasts a few minutes, just until Orlando can reply: "You little American fucker. I can't do that. We love each other and love's a bitch. That's why I write her poems, letters, take photographs for her. I send them to her new place. We fight until we bleed, but I swear we love each other. You little American fucker, our love's just a bitch like that."

And he smiles. Henry never reacts well. People say he's got a short fuse. Orlando and I say otherwise. Henry is a good guy; in his words, "big and tender, but with a woman's heart." Still, Henry wrestles the bear away from Orlando and calmly responds: "Dear poet, my dearest photographer, my little slice of sugarbread, suffer all you can, suffer as much as you wish. It will do you good. It will serve some purpose. Believe me, you'll see. People will see it in everything you do and no one will think of it as art. You'll let go of everything, and what you make will be your own life. You'll mix it together just to vomit it back up again on paper. You don't feel like you belong anywhere. We're alone, fucked and dead. A city or a country isn't anything but a big construct. Paris, America, London. What are they? Metaphors. It's that real. It's that simple. Go back to Jamy's cunt if you can. Slide back into her vagina. Bite her ovaries and then fall asleep there. Crawl back into her uterus. But do it in other holes, too. Never get tied down anywhere. Ahmel, did you hear me? I'm telling you, it's healthy. Really healthy. But be careful, you have a good wife."

I watch them wrestle. I watch them there, taking up all the space on my bed, each touching Teddy-Honey's fur. I watch them there, with their dicks so hard they're about to explode, drooling, their eyes nowhere. I watch them there, moaning "Jamy," moaning "Tania," as they touch their hard dicks. And all I can do is watch.

I'm in the corner. Lost. If Henry hadn't made that speech I would, like other times, want to touch Teddy-Honey with my hard-on, with my pants bulging, drooling, just like they are. But their words are lodged in my mind. I don't feel like moaning "Yani." My head, my arms, my legs don't respond. I'm lost. Maybe I'm even dead.

So I watch them, unmoving, marooned in the corner of my room. This is why Yani thinks we're a trio of queers. But what does it matter? Not many people come by who I can really talk to. Or almost no one. Or no one. All my friends have gone away. If it weren't for Yani, Vania and Edith my life would be one big void. I would be an enormous piece of shit. Or maybe I am, but at least I still have the spirit to invent a life for myself together with my wife. Or maybe I am, but I still wish I was one of the Three Good Soldiers, and that we could watch each other's backs, even though in reality Edith and Vania would carry most of the weight. Or maybe I'm a real piece of shit, and that's why I fall helplessly into tangos, boleros, tears and alcohol when I remember that the Three Good Soldiers couldn't bring the blade down on reality, overturn it once and for all.

"We're up against the ropes." That's the only thing Vania, Edith and I heard that day at the apartment. Edith said it when we had stopped crying. We all hugged and I left. Time, life and our metaphor of a country are wearing me down. I bleed, I cry, my nose will break, I'll lose all my teeth. My bones will disappear and I'll end up a sack of soft shit. And around me people will pass by as if nothing were happening. I wanted to do something, but didn't know what. Henry was right, we Three Good Soldiers were alone, fucked and dead.

What could I do besides listen to these two run their mouths? What could I do besides pay some attention to these two ghosts, let them come into my room and convince Yani to let them play with the teddy bear? Something had to happen after Henry's speech. If something happened it would mean they had lit a spark. Then I don't know what—I'd have to sprinkle the gunpowder all over the city or something. I feel like a whore, always waiting for Orlando and Henry to come fuck me with their words, to light the spark in this ball of fat I have for a head. I am a whore. And if it all blows up, I'll have a giant orgasm, just like a fucking mare in heat.

After they fought over the bear, after they grew fed up with thinking about Jamy and Tania, they'd stretch their skin and show me pieces of their muscles, photos, tidbits from the literary world or parts of the books they were trying to write. Some people looked at them with suspicion. Sometimes I wonder whether they do it for attention or if they really are incendiary. Orlando and Henry despise the cream we're all floating around in. *Everything is fake,* they say. *This is a world of bastards and censors.* They're like two old *vedettes.* They like to clear away shit, wave away the flies, dynamite the stable that shelters the sacred cows. Squeezing Honey's little arms, Orlando says: "*Morenito, necesitamos una* bad writing, pages and pages of writing. Ahmel Ahmel, pray to all the saints for bad writing to appear all over the place. *La necesitamos,* my little doll. We just need a bad writing. All we need is a bad writing for breaking the literary pulp. What do you think of that, old man?"

Henry eyes him. He tries to wrestle the bear away and then whispers in my ear that our dear Orlando is a real son of a bitch, but a clever one, who knows very well that the question lies in its limits:

"It's a big mistake to contain yourself. Have you ever asked yourself what art is, clever guy?"

"To put a bullet in something?" I ask.

Henry looks at me, winks, and says I won some points, but not all of them.

"My little brown doll, art is nothing but a few drops of laxative—not many, but just enough to make you poop and give you a good cleaning out," Orlando says. "Ahmel Ahmel, if you shoot a gun someone should die. You have to aim for the head. And shoot."

What could I do besides listen to them? I never say much. I hide a lot, what I can, of my projects. Even though Orlando invites me to do things, to collaborate (a series of photographs and a book and a half lie among my papers), I hide most of it. Maybe it's because I don't know when I'll be able to share my stuff without feeling embarrassed, without thinking about what I'm lacking, what I can't say to both of them: "Son of a bitch shitheads, stop fucking around, stop masturbating and tell me what you think of this." Sometimes I think my interest in literature and photography is a hobby I need to drop but that I can't bring myself to put a bullet in, to send my reality flying into pieces.

I need Orlando and Henry. Sometimes they'll call me to put off their visit:
"No, nothing's wrong dear. If we're not coming it's only so we don't get stuck in a routine."
"No, nothing's wrong, Ahmel Ahmel. I can't bear the thought of killing the spirit of our meetings."

It really seems as if they plan their visits together, though they claim they don't. I often suspect the problem isn't really routine, because sometimes Orlando's voice will sound gritty, wet, as if he has just worn it out on a long crying session, in a falsetto voice, howling "Jamy." Or sometimes I'll hear the sound of a camera shutter, or the soft snaking of his pen against a notepad, or the keys of a computer, or the masked voice that Henry uses to tell me he's not coming, and I can hear in the background a sound like a cat, soft moans, a quiet whimpering, and his voice murmuring "Tania," "Irene," "Honey," "Iona," or the sound of a blunt object, a pen, a pencil, slithering across a smooth surface: a blank sheet of paper, a notepad, Tania's, Irene's, Iona's skin.

More than speak with them, I try to listen to the phone connection, drink in the noises on the line to find out how much truth—or lies—is contained in their voices. They'll call, they'll say it's to avoid this country's terrible cycle that's dragging us all down.

They scare me. When the phone rings, my legs go. I tremble. All because of one word: routine. Just hearing it reminds me that I'm facing the void. And it's not far off. After their call, tango, boleros, tears and alcohol leave me in a bad way. I don't manage to do a thing. I'm nothingness. I'm a baby thrown out on the hot asphalt in the middle of the road. Naked. A baby with skin, muscle and bones mashed under wheels and footsteps, covered in soot, dust, spit and cigarette butts.

If I don't get one of these calls, the day passes as if it were a field of freshly-mowed grass. As if Yani and I were lolling in the grass. Fucking one, two, three, a thousand, a million times. As if I had decided to graze a while, shit in the shade and go to sleep. Tranquility. Nothing but tranquility on this soft carpet that isn't a call from Orlando or Henry.

But they call. And my legs tremble. To face the day. To face life, far, so far away, too far away from that endless grass carpet. Orlando and Henry speak almost at the same time. I give each one a chance.

I tell them not to worry if I don't respond. I always try to explain that my phone is new and I can speak with both of them at the same time. "Are you still there, O?"

"Yes, Ahmel Ahmel."

"Are you still there, H?"

"Of course, my dear."

"Ahmel Ahmel, I called to say I'm not coming this afternoon."

"Ahmel, I called to say I'm not coming this afternoon."

I don't respond. My legs tremble. They're not coming.

The bed will remain mine. Terribly mine. The room will remain mine. Terribly mine. Teddy-Honey will only be Teddy. Just my dear, fuzzy, honey-colored bear. Yani's teddy bear. The day won't be the same. It's the warning call.

"Hey, are you still there, doll of good intentions? Are you still there, dear? Say something, please. Speak, my doll. Answer me, my dear."

"When will you come?"

"You know, soon."

"When? When? Please!"

"Soon, you'll see. Say hi to Honey. Say hi to Yani."

Orlando wrote in my notebook: *Start from zero, again and again. An eternal cycle. Every ten years. Again and again. Start from zero.*

Orlando thinks this is our reality. An unreal reality: "Ahmel Ahmel, everything happens between blinks: clips of reality, sequence shots of irreality, a reel of photographs that lasts for ten years to be replaced by another that lasts for ten years. Then all you can do is start from a new year zero which, in the end, is the same one that begins all cycles."

So it seems Orlando has returned. I feel a surge of energy. I think I can hear him. He whispers that this decade thing is The Answer. "Only this, my doll, nothing else. The answer to every question, no matter what, the hard and endless cycle of ten."

He tells me to pay attention, to read the papers: "Give the headlines a good look, my little brown doll, slice into the front page and then read the same headlines."

Orlando wants me to have a good look at the faces of passersby, in the city, in the streets, on the statues: "Look hard, Ahmel Ahmel, the same gestures alternating between happiness and pain, the child who is born, the old man who dies, the headlines tattooed on people's skin; the crimson and gashes tattooed on their skin; the need for sex and desperation tattooed on their skin; the rain, the sun, the breeze and the saltpeter tattooed on their skin, then guillotine it all and look again."

So we live in irreality. Castles of playing cards under the sun, machined wood, hopes, shingles, heartbreak, security fences, colonnades, deceptions, arcades, happiness, shit and dog piss. Playing cards scrutinizing everything, governing everything, mixing up everything. "If something is real, it's this cycle that ends every ten years. And we'll go back to zero, my doll of good intentions. Eternally."

And should we care about time? Orlando says we unlive a long and painful eternity that ends when our bones give out. So it's not time that should matter to us, but timelessness. That's what Henry thinks. "The real cancer is time. It's eating us away. The cancer of time is eating us away."

Henry makes me pay attention to everything I see, he says it's necessary, that nothing is more important: "Look, *muchacho*, what do you see? Nothing will change. Our heroes have killed themselves or are killing themselves. What do you see? Should we care about time? The hero, then, is not Time, but Timelessness."

And the rest, Henry? What happened to the rest? And the rest, Orlando? What happened before my real day zero, the beginning of my cycle?

Orlando says The Answer can apply to everything. Henry expects me to not let any details slip by. "I already told that clever guy. Don't forget it either, Ahmel. Find what was left out of the books. We're no longer innocent enough to believe the poets and sit around the table in the evenings, to invoke the spirits of the dead."

Then what should I do, Henry M.? Then what should I do, Orlando L.?

I feel Henry's presence like a surge of energy. It sends me spinning. It floats to the bookcase. It knocks my papers, my photographs to the floor. It searches for my notebook. Though I only assume it was his presence that made everything fall, and not Yani, when she tripped on the bookcase. The notebook fell open: *"The age demands violence, but we are getting only abortive explosions."*

There was more in that note that I took from Henry. There was more. As if the passion had burned up in its escape, as if we couldn't propose anything that wouldn't last for more than a day. And really, that's what I am. I'm nothing like a Good Soldier. I think I'm the one who burned up in the escape.

Unnerved, I look right, then left. I feel that surge of energy. I walk to the window. I see playing cards. One on top of the other. And the wind that insists on blowing between calm and calm. Sometimes hard. Like a hurricane. *Dear God, Henry, and the rest of it? For the love of God, Orlando, where did the rest of it go?*

The phone rings. My legs are trembling again. It's Orlando. It's Henry.

"Are you at the window, Ahmel Ahmel? Are you standing in front of the window, *muchacho*?"

I can't speak, or move.

"You've got me worried, dear. I called Orlando and we spoke about you. Are you there?"

"Don't leave me hanging. I just called our little American and we spoke for a long, long, long time. Are you there?"

"Yes."

"Yani and Honey too?"

"Yes. For now."

"What is that supposed to mean? For the love of God, get out from in front of that window. Get the fuck out from in front of that window and go down to the street." "Good luck, dear. You know what to do."

"Take care, Ahmel Ahmel. Try to make sure nothing happens to your girl, you know how lucky you are, she's the best girl in the world."

"Yani Yani is the most lovely and sensible girl in the world. Look into her eyes. Listen to her once, for fuck's sake. Then go down to the street. Do it, please, please."

"Ok."

"You're a good boy. Did you know that? We're lucky to have you." "What would we do without your room? Without our meetings? They're a blessing." "You're very quiet."

"Maybe that's healthy."

"You should start writing already."

"Ok Henry, will we see each other some other day?"
"Ok Orlando, will we see each other some other day? Will we see each other? Will we?"

"Goodbye. Get out from in front of that window and get started. *Ciao, ciao, mon amour.*"
"*Adiós*, my little doll."
"*Ciao, ciao, je t'aime.*"

Yani is in bed. She is stroking Teddy. She strokes him a long while. Until her eyes come to rest on nothing, and she begins to utter unconnected words. Until she appears to be drooling, and she murmurs "Ahmel." Until her hand ungrasps everything, and falls from her body. She doesn't look at me. Her hand slowly creeps, like an animal, over and into my skin. I look at her. I think I can hear Henry's voice in falsetto. The surge of energy says today is a good day to first have a roll with my wife and then clear up a few things. It says—and its voice grows louder now—that I will find a use for everything, everything. "When you're done messing around, sing. Not too off key, of course. It will do you good. Then listen to everything your wife has to say."

Yani is still lying in bed. She's taking up all the space. Yani and Teddy-Honey. I think of H's words, O's words, the notebook, the camera. *Routine, violence, abortive explosions, metaphor, headlines, irreality, heroes, timelessness, horror.* What are we in all of this? Figures on a canvas? Figures and nothing more?

"Leave all that for later," Yani says.

And we roll around in the bed until we're nothing more than a mass. Tongue, phallus, sweat, vulva, saliva. Almost dying.

"Go get your wallet, I'll put in all the money I have too," says Yani, still gasping.

"What are you doing?"

"Helping you. Helping me. I might know you better than I know myself. We need scissors and newspapers. What are we if not figures? Tomorrow we'll go out early and buy all the press we can. Why don't we go sit under the ceiba tree in the Parque de la Fraternidad?"

The image of Orlando appears. It crosses my frontal cortex and stops just on the other side of the door, leaning in, peeking its head through. I blush just thinking about it. Could he keep this secret? If he were here, he'd say: "I don't know if I can, Ahmel Ahmel, I just want to launch myself over this city, and grow wings, and fly and tell everyone to go to the Parque de la Fraternidad, that I don't know why or what for, but to go. But who would believe me anyway, if everything is pure irreality?"

Orlando's image rolls up the sleeves of his pullover, smiles, and says: "*Muchachito*, the little American and I were right."

We scraped together sixty pesos. On our way to the park we bought forty newspapers and six magazines. When we got there we sat in the shade of the giant ceiba.

"Take these," says Yani, handing me a pair of scissors.

"What should I do?"

"Cut what you want."

Yani divides the stacks of newspapers and magazines between us:

"Don't watch what I do. Do what you want."

I begin to cut strange figures. I mutilate images, headlines, blocks of meaningless text, until I finally remember the first real act of illusionism I ever saw: my kindergarten teacher multiplied a single sheet of blue paper into a chain of little men. Then she passed out pages from the newspaper so we could practice. It was funny to watch our hands, small and clumsy, as they spawned these grotesque bodies, covered in red and black ink and images of natural disasters, editorials, leaders, criminals, headlines, cartoons and armed conflicts.

For us it was like a party to breed those little monstrosities, to cut into pieces the newspapers that our parents kept out of our reach until the day's end. It was like a party to see all those bodies hand in hand. And I for one saw myself cut, together with all the other children, into those newspaper pages.

With each snip the little dolls become even funnier. Dozens of repeated figures, hand in hand, with hats, skirts, pants, in different positions. Women and men simply standing, or frozen mid-jump, with their hands and legs in the air, or linked face to face, cheek to cheek, fist to fist, or holding guns linked barrel to barrel, or in an angry stance, as if they were about to fight.

I don't want to look at Yani. And I hear the *snip snip* of her scissors. I want to surprise her. I want her figures to surprise me. One page, and another, and another. But it's really hard, and it's not just pages I am cutting. Each headline, each image, each article is a blow, one that sends me reeling back to the apartment where Vania, Edith and I were naked, drifting, drowning in boleros, memories, alcohol and tangos. We never again spoke of what happened. We never again spoke of how we were up against the ropes, even though we never stopped taking thousands of blows. We were the Three Good Soldiers, but to say it was to expose a vulnerability.

And it was through this vulnerability that reality crept into our reality, or irreality crept into our reality. How to rearrange it once and for all? How to put a bullet in it? Those were the eternal questions that I, at least, kept asking. And as if the act of cutting a long chain of humans would again become that one true act of illusionism, the front page of the newspaper in my hands became a kiss repeated among dozens of little men, dozens of women. I cut naked ones, breast to breast, phallus to phallus. I closed and opened the chain, so the bodies would touch completely. An orgy of paper men. A tangle of tits, legs, lips and dicks. Endless copulation. Maybe a true and total brotherhood.

The constant *snip snip* of Yani's scissors is intriguing. She told me to cut what I wanted, without looking at her. But the surge of energy that sometimes surrounds me when I feel the presence of Orlando and Henry forces me to spy on her. "Helping you. Helping me."

Yani had said she wanted to help herself and help me at the same time. She had known what she wanted from the beginning. She's also cutting chains of little men. She had been doing it since the very moment we sat down in the park. A group of people begins to gather around us. I tell her,

"Help me pass this out," and Yani opens her backpack.

We had scissors and a good amount of newspapers. The magazines are still intact. We explain that they'll have to share the scissors, but that there's paper for everyone. We ask them to cut without looking at what anyone else is doing, unless they can't think of anything, and then it's ok. Some prefer to look. Others ask for scissors, including Vania and Edith.

"What a surprise," I say, as I pass them some scissors. "Where were you off to?"

"To here." Edith lets go of Vania's hand, greets me with a hug and a kiss on the cheek and then says hello to Yani.

"You didn't spread the word through your friend Orlando? It would have been a good idea," Vania says, giving me a kiss and a hug, then saying hello to Yani. "What will we do with all the cutouts?"

"We'll see."

Vania and Edith hardly have time to sit down. Two police officers cut through the group of people gathered under the ceiba tree.

"Who is in charge here?" one officer asks.

"No one," I say. "I didn't have anything to do and came to the park with some scissors and newspapers. The people appeared on their own. Maybe they didn't have anything to do either."

Everyone stops cutting. Some walk away when the police aren't looking. They're free to go as they came.

"Who brought the scissors and papers?"

"I did."

"So you did have something to do. This isn't the kind of thing you do to kill time."

The older of the two officers asks for my identification. They speak among themselves and on their radios. I look at Yani, concerned. Yani looks at me, concerned. Vania and Edith look at us, walk to the center of the group, embrace and begin to make out. They're both dressed in white. Light fabric, nearly transparent, which sometimes clings to the curves of their bodies.

Vania is wearing a short white top that shows off her flat, tattooed abdomen. Two women with white skin in white clothes. They look like two pieces of marble on the park tiles. The fabric against their skin. White on white. Embracing. The tattoo, which sometimes slips under the white fabric, behind Edith's body. It's a long kiss. A very long kiss. A kiss so long it sucks at their lipstick and the officers' gazes.

Someone says in my ear that these are two crafty chicks: "The one with the tattoo is a cat and the other is a fox. Two little animals. Look how tender they are. The whores. Everyone wants to bang them, dear, men and women. Do you realize what they're up to?"

It's the voice of Henry, who has just arrived. Orlando told him. He says that all this—gesturing toward Vania and Edith—is more than a kiss, just like the newspaper cutouts are more than figures. "What a great idea. You're a very clever boy. Look at everyone, but keep those officers in sight, their dicks are about to explode. Who wouldn't be able to say anything about this? Will they forget about it? Let's hope so. You need to brace yourself, my dear, the worst is still to come."

I don't know why he says it's a good try, though I do know that something is about to get out of hand and the worst is still to come. "My dear, have you ever gotten hard looking at a statue or a paper cutout? Have you felt it? I've seen it all: your cutouts, your girlfriends, and my dick is about to explode. Take care of those girls like you take care of your Yani, those three are the best girls in the world. You know it."

Do I know it, Henry? Does the *morenito* know what's happening? This is a performance, baby. A bad writing, disobedient bodies, impudent hands and heads destroying dozens of newspapers, baby. They'll have to punish you. This is shit. Ahmel Ahmel, no bad examples in public. Do you remember that bullet? Well you put it in those two men in uniform. Look between their legs. They won't let you off for this.

Orlando also tells me the worst is still to come. I look into the officers' eyes. I look at their hands, their zippers. I listen to their radios. They clear their throats. They adjust their berets, their guns. They put away their walkie-talkies and, as they approach, hide their immense bulges under their ticket books.

"Citizen, come with us."

"For cutting newspapers?"

"We'll explain everything in the office."

"Citizen," say O and H in my ear, "citizen, ask them what they mean by *everything*. You need to know what they say. You can do it. Remember, you're a citizen."

Yani whispers for me to say nothing: "Just go with them. What can they accuse you of besides cutting papers and littering in the park?"

The officers look at me, speak in low voices and I think I can hear them say that I am enough, that I am the one who organized everything and that the place will empty out in less than half an hour. They gesture toward their patrol car. The younger of the two asks what they should do with Vania and Edith.

"There's nothing we can do."

And it was true. To do anything with them would be impossible.

The group of people makes way. The officers take my ID card, a few chains of little men and a newspaper. They quickly scan the group and linger on Henry's hissing, Orlando's smile, Yani's wide eyes and the long, long kiss between Vania and Edith that they still won't quit.

We get in the car. The group in the park turns toward it. They don't let it out of their sight. The younger officer is at the wheel. He looks at me, and then his partner. There is a hard plastic shield between us. They speak in low tones and the older officer signals.

The tires squeal. To reach the station, we have to drive around the park. No one has budged. Vania and Edith leave the group and walk around the ceiba tree, hand in hand, without losing sight of the patrol car. They follow us. They know the officers are watching them in the rearview; they stop, come together in a long embrace, of which only a trace remains in my memory, and perhaps that of the officers.

How to guillotine reality, how to cut into it and rearrange it? This is my eternal question. I have it lodged in my brain like a tumor, a goddamned tumor that takes up all the space. There are days I can't forget it.

I called Henry and Orlando. I'm scared. Every morning someone leaves a chain of little men at my door. I live on the fifth floor, and no one sees a thing. No one knows a thing. They appear right on my doorstep. I'm no fucking hero. I know that since I left the station no one has done anything similar in the park again. So then who could it be?

It wasn't Vania or Edith. They tell me. For over a month now they've been getting arrow-pierced hearts and flowers. No one has seen a thing. Edith says she doesn't know what to do. Vania can't take it anymore. She has a ticket to Canada, one-way. They know it will be a long time before they see each other again. I'm scared too, very scared.

I began to write things down, scratching things out like a lunatic, not letting anything escape my sight. Now there's nothing left of the Three Good Soldiers. We wanted to carry a load and it exploded in our hands. We flew off in pieces. We're fragments that can hardly be rebuilt within Cuba. Splinters.

What can you make with a pile of splinters? Nothing. Henry, Orlando and Yani say otherwise. "We'll make something out of this trash, we'll do a lot with all this rubble, you'll see, little splintered doll, you'll see everything and it will all be clearer. Don't turn into a little bitch and stay that way like a fucked lunatic. You know you'll encounter the void wherever you go, it will be there, waiting for you. Everything is pure fiction, nothing but metaphor. *Nene*, talk to me, let me help you. Don't stop, I'll help you gather all those cutouts they leave at your door. You'll see you were right, they'll serve for something."

Yani is in my room. She's lying on the bed with Teddy-Honey between her legs. She's purring "Ahmel" as I look over the figures that have appeared at the door.

"I don't know what all this means."

"You look tired. Look at the circles under your eyes. Leave all that for now. Come here. I'll tell you more later."

I look at her. She plays with the bear. Teddy-Honey looks like he's enjoying the game. Yani sits him on her belly. She begins to softly stroke him. Until one of her hands falls from her body. It goes off on its own. Crawling all over my skin. "Come here," and she traps me. And we roll around on the bed until we are nothing but a mass. Tongue, phallus, sweat, vulva, saliva. One, two, three times. Almost dying.

"There's no order to splinters," says Yani, between gasps. "What happened to the Three Good Soldiers? What do you know of me, Orlando, Henry? *Nene*, you know the whole story."

Yani had it all clear from the beginning. Chaos, pain, boredom, death, games, horror. Vania, Edith and me, that's what we were. Orlando, Henry, Yani and me, that's what we were. We were facing reality. Alone. Like many. Adrift over the void, always on the verge of running aground. Surrounded by people, in the midst of the bustling city, with nothing but ourselves for company. We really were alone, fucked and dead.

Yani hands me a notebook. She brings me a pen. She marks an X on a blank page and says: "Do you dare? Start here."

I close the book. I say I'm sorry.

I hardly have the strength to respond.

Havana Light
LIEN CARRAZANA LAU

> *To try curing someone of a "vice," of what is the deepest thing he has, is to attack his very being, and this is indeed how he himself understands it, since he will never forgive you for wanting him to destroy himself in your way and not his.*
> Tears and Saints,
> EMIL CIORAN

I was twelve years old the first time I put a cigarette to my lips. Ileana would steal them from her grandmother and bring them to school, hidden in her pencil box. We'd smoke them at my house in the dining room. Alone together, we'd cough and blow smoke from our noses and mouths. Then we'd wrap the butts in notebook paper and throw them out onto the roof.

We smoked that way for a while, hidden from everyone, stealing cigarettes from anyone we could. Sometimes, if we wanted some flavor, we'd rub them in Chinese menthol, and then pretend we were motorcycle chicks, movie stars, famous singers; that we were older. We'd hide the stench with perfume.

In high school I'd smoke the cigarettes I got from boys at parties, and especially from the boys I liked. I thought it was sexy to lift the cigarette to my lips, look into someone's eyes and say, in English, "Have you got a light?"

The sentence had a hypnotic effect; very few girls knew English at the time. The boy in question would give me a light, and I'd inhale deeply and blow the smoke back into his face, just like I'd seen in so many movies; then I'd offer him the cigarette, stained with my lipstick.

The method never failed. Thanks to cigarettes I was always quite popular with the boys. I was also lucky enough to look older than I was, which meant I could buy cigarettes in any café without getting strange looks. I would buy them with whatever was left over from my allowance. I'd smoke hidden from my parents, at school, at parties, during outings.

In the years leading up to university, smoking helped me concentrate for exams during those late nights I'd stay up studying. It would relax me when I was overwhelmed by exams, loves, uncomfortable school dorms and my desire to escape from everything, to be in my house, comfortable, protected, coddled. The cigarette kept me company when I missed the streets of my neighborhood, Santos Suárez, and the view of the city from Loma del Burro.

The cigarette was where I hid when any situation reached its limits and being a social individual became more complicated than mathematics. The cigarette gave me strength, helped me carry the weight of the days and encouraged me with its trail of smoke: "Don't give up."

During a break from school my mother caught me smoking in the bathroom. I threw the butt into the toilet, but it was no use: the smoke gave me away. My parents were hysterical. No one smoked in my house. My parents are doctors and campaign against smoking with an inordinate obsession. I suspect it has something to do with my grandfather on my father's side, of whom no one ever speaks, even though a photograph of him holding a cigar is still displayed on a shelf in our house.

The day they caught me smoking, my father, who was very ethical in his medical practice, forgot about his prevention work and punished me severely. They didn't let me go out with my friends. They wouldn't give me any money.

When the lockdown was over, I began to bum cigarettes from everyone, smoking constantly, lighting one after the other. When I couldn't get my hands on whole cigarettes, I'd join them together, or gut them and roll the tobacco in rice paper. I even smoked the bits in a pipe my friend gave me.

If I couldn't find anyone to give me a cigarette, I'd sell something: a book, clothes. When I didn't have anything to sell, I'd ask to borrow money from my grandparents on my mother's side. I'd lie and say it was for notebooks. When I couldn't find anyone to give me money, I'd try to find a boyfriend who smoked; I wanted to intoxicate myself with nicotine, to rebel against my parents' dogma.

My greatest victory was turning sixteen. That's when I informed my parents I would no longer be reprimanded for my habit. I would smoke freely under their inquisitive stares, their only request being that I didn't smoke anywhere near them. I deemed their wish reasonable and accepted it. I was free, and no longer had to hide like a bandit just to savor my morning coffee along with the smoke of my Populars.

University was a paradise in terms of emancipation: to smoke the universe late into the night, to smoke love, aloneness, sex, youth. To smoke until Havana became a blur through the smoke. With the money from my first job as a translator, I had switched from the "lungcrushers" to the filtered Populars. I loved to softly bite the filter as I lit the end; the yellow filter between my lips only enhanced my cool look.

It was through smoking that I met Néstor. We had both taken refuge from a downpour under the arcades at the Plaza de Armas. He approached me to ask for a light. I handed him my lighter and he proceeded to light a white cigarette while I observed the box, which was blue: Hollywood Lights. "You can tell a smoker by their face," he said, handing back my lighter. "Yeah? So you're saying I have cigarette written all over my face?" I laughed. "No, you have nostalgia written all over your face," he replied.

Then we watched the rain in silence. I took out a cigarette and lit it. "The way you smell the cigarette just before you put it between your lips, the way you breathe in when you light it, as if you wanted to inhale the panorama, the trees, the cobblestones, the way you draw it away from your lips, looking dazed at the sky, the rain, and breathing out a city transformed into smoke . . . you're savoring nostalgia," he said, and I just stood there, staring at him without saying a word.

Only then I inhaled. "There you go again. You have a voracious appetite. Now you're trying to smoke up this idiot who is interrupting you as you enjoy your solitary pleasure of lightness."

"No, no, what you said was beautiful," I replied, sorry that he had noticed I was dazed, "really beautiful," and I smiled. Minutes later, we were savoring our coffee in a nearby bar.

A month later I had moved into his house. Néstor lived alone in a penthouse in an old building right by the Malecón. His ex-wife had gone off to a writers' conference in Bucharest and never came back. He spent almost a year isolating himself in his attic until one day, for some strange reason, he fell in love with me.

Maybe it was my hips, the way they looked in the tight low-rise jeans I was wearing that afternoon; my cleavage; or my high cheekbones, which might have reminded him of that bitch who left him in Havana with a wardrobe full of dresses, a stack of poems dedicated to him and a taste for the smooth cigarettes she used to smoke. Maybe he had just run out of reasons to keep thinking about her. Maybe it was all of that, or none of it, but ultimately it was the realization that we both saw things through the prism of nostalgia, the same prism that kept us from leaving Cuba and the streets, friends, books, parks, the smell of Cuban tobacco, the food, Santa María beach, the Morro lighthouse, the sound of the cannon every night at nine, and so many other things that made up the city that was so unique and ours.

During that time my smoking habit was clinched. I smoked a pack a day. I'd buy them in cartons so I'd never run out. Néstor kept smoking his lights, and I'd tease him. "You smoke like a Barbie, you and your slims. You're not a real smoker, you're a lightweight, the same as the tourists I work with."

Néstor would say that one day I'd understand, that one day I'd smoke lights, that in this city cigarettes were what really activated nostalgia, cigarettes were oppressing Havana. "Nonsense, Havana is oppressing my Populars, my Populars that smell and taste like a real cigarette, and not that insipid thing you smoke that doesn't even have a decent name. Hollywood. Maybe if you lived in Los Angeles. But no, my dear, you live smack in the center of Havana, and here we say 'I'm Cuban, I'm popular,'" I would reply, citing the slogan on the pack.

Even if we could never agree on brands, we did agree on how much we liked the canescent color of the smoke, the pleasure of a drink, a good book and a coffee, always always always with a cigarette between our fingers. Smoking distracted us during the long nights of blackouts, when the heat kept us out on the terrace until dawn. Smoking made us less apathetic about going out, about not wanting to mix with the sea of people that flooded the buses, the breadlines, the pizzerias. Smoking was all we had left to evade the harshness we could sense in the walls, the buildings, the faces of the people, the echo of their voices projected in the air, their tears shed in the corridors of the airport.

"We'll be the ones to switch off the lights at the Morro. The last ones left," I said to Néstor as we counted how many friends we had seen off.

"No, you and I will turn the lights back on after the last Cuban turns them off," he replied, taking out his lighter to light another cigarette.

I lit one too and blew smoke over him, and he tried to defend himself by blowing back the soft smoke from his lights. We started to play until we ended in an embrace, sweating and moaning. To make love and smoke. To smoke and make love. That's how we killed time and how we were happy, that's how we survived the tedium of an agonizing city.

One day I emptied out one of his aromatic cigarettes and filled it with my stronger tobacco. He smoked it while he read on the terrace, as I died laughing, hiding in the kitchen. When he finished it he came over to me: "Do you think I've liked lights all my life? I used to smoke like you, I used to smoke to crush my lungs and kill my pain."

"What pain are you talking about, Néstor? You're crazy. My husband is crazy," and I turned away and began to strip my clothes off as I held a cigarette, hoping he would follow me and, like other times, end up tangled in the bed with me, making love and smoking. It excited him to see me smoking and indifferent as I allowed him to penetrate me.

So Néstor went and got a cigarette—a real light one this time—lit it and followed me, but then he stopped in the middle of the living room. He had a coughing fit that ended with him spitting blood on the floor. I got scared. I brought him water. I pounded him on the back. I rubbed him gently. I said it was my fault for giving him one of my cigarettes. He said that the smoke had gone down the "wrong tube" and that I wasn't to blame.

But the cough kept coming back. More blood-laced spit convinced him to go see my father.

My parents didn't like to visit us. The house, according to them, was a giant ashtray. When he saw us there at his office, my father looked concerned, but didn't lecture me; he conducted himself like an excellent doctor. He ordered analyses, x-rays, and made an appointment to go over the results.

We went back a few days later. My father was very obliging, which was not like him. He received us, along with another doctor, and asked me to stay in the waiting room. I lit another cigarette to pass the time, but a nurse quickly reproached me: "You can't smoke in the hospital, you have to go out front." As if I hadn't seen them a thousand times smoking in the bathrooms, in their locker rooms, in the cafeteria, on the patio.

I went out to the park, bought a newspaper from the kiosk, and sat on a bench to finish my cigarette in peace. A man with pens in the pockets of his shirt and a briefcase in his hand sat down at the other end of the bench. I had just tossed out the end of my cigarette, which was still glowing off and on, the yellow filter stained with my lipstick. The man with the pens looked at me and smiled, revealing his blackened teeth. Startled, I looked away and went back to reading. The man placed his briefcase on the ground and looked at me again.

I followed his movements out of the corner of my eye, concealed behind the newspaper. Then he opened his briefcase, reached inside and, when he drew out his hand he was holding my cigarette between his fingers. He inhaled with desperation as I stared at his dirty fingernails, his yellowed fingers. I looked at my own fingers: they weren't so yellow, but they smelled of pure nicotine. Were my teeth yellow too?

I took a mirror from my purse and inspected my teeth. They were a little yellow. I thought about the man's mouth, his lips as they pressed into the filter stained with my lipstick, his stained teeth as they filtered the smoke from that drag that must have tasted like Popular tobacco, dirt, lipstick and me. I felt as if this specimen with his rotten teeth were putting his mouth on me. Disgusted, I stood up and walked back to the hospital.

Néstor was standing in the office door speaking to my father. "Well, what is it?" I asked him, anxious. He didn't respond, and my father went on about having us over for dinner that weekend, which was strange: I didn't understand why he was suddenly being so nice. I said goodbye to him and dragged Néstor toward the exit.

He was carrying an envelope in his hands with the results. "Dammit Néstor, will you just tell me what you have already?" I said, irritated. "The nostalgia disease, that's what I have. Let's go home. I'm tired," and he looked so sad I didn't press him.

When we got home he said he wanted to shower. He kissed me and closed himself in the bathroom. I immediately found the envelope. I pulled out the x-ray and held it up to the light. I moved to the window for even more light, but couldn't see anything besides two black stains that looked like giant branches. I found the paper with the results, and the pain—that pain Néstor had spoken of—surged up, took over my body.

I collapsed to the floor, my eyes tearing up and my saliva thick: I needed a cigarette. I looked to my Populars, which were on the table next to the Hollywood Lights in their blue box, blue like nostalgia. I took a Light from the box. I smelled it. I brought it to my lips. I lit it, watching the red ring burn the paper, leaving a cylindrical ashen layer behind it. It tasted of nothing, but even nothingness tastes like something, and this cigarette reminded me of that lightness where I let myself go, where I float like a dry leaf over the half-lit streets of Havana. A dry leaf that's afraid of being crushed by the heavy footstep of some passerby. That must be why Néstor and I took refuge on that rooftop, so no one would stomp us into dust.

I walked toward the door to the terrace and looked out at the city lights, which came on one by one as the sun went down. I exhaled smoke and night fell behind it. I knew the pain running through me was a fact I would have to face, that cigarettes were only traps, waiting for me in some cafeteria, in some bar, in some afternoon where the atrocious lightness of this city falls over me. I knew why light cigarettes were the only ones that could match the emptiness I feel when I watch as Havana dies under my feet and no one cares. That's why we smoke: to forget, to ease the pain, so that it can go on hurting and we don't care. But now I know that pain—be what it may—cannot be eased with more pain.

I put out the cigarette. Néstor still hadn't come out of the bathroom. I gathered all of the cigarettes in the house, including Néstor's. I threw them all in a bag and was about to throw it in the trash, but I stopped: some homeless person might have found them. So I went out to the terrace, took an old can and emptied the cigarettes into it. I sprinkled it with alcohol and sent the nostalgia up in flames. I watched as the light fire devoured smiles, games, embraces, conversations, nights that Néstor and I would never live again.

I looked up at the city, some lights had just come on around the Malecón, others went out like cigarette butts. The smell of nicotine filled the air. I closed my eyes and focused on the smell, as if I were rewinding a song over and over, so I could hear its happy refrain just one more time, just one more time. I desperately wanted to smoke.

I could see myself running downstairs, down to the nearest café, and asking in a near-whisper: "A pack of cigarettes, please." I could see the woman behind the counter open her mouth to ask which brand. I saw myself pointing through the glass: "The light blue ones, blue like nostalgia."

I opened my eyes to see Néstor standing in the door.

The flames died away.

Skhizein (Decalogue for the Year Zero)
POLINA MARTÍNEZ SHVIÉTSOVA

1.
Each being is the one most distant from itself.
NIETZSCHE

The formula for mystery is insanity. Lucidity as a process of emanation, a flux of adolescent lividness: a heart murmur. The intangible memory of the desert and a future litany when weary eyelids begin to flutter, almost unaware. I am me.

Texts pass through my fingers and I feel the naked contortions of death. I'm at the edge of something, the summit of nothing. The violence of my open sex has me bent over with laughter and smelling holy, of *semen*tery and saliva. I am alive.

A terrible plain bleeds on the palate of my happy anguish. Everything sounds like purple blood, like wet viscera about to explode. I go, I come.

My tongue tied by thousands of failures still resists: they are the death rattles of a miracle, where salvation and glory are still possible. I am insane, but I am me. We are insane, but the formula for this insanity will always remain a mystery.

2.

This hour that can arrive sometimes outside of all hours,
a hole in the net of time, this way of being between,
not above or behind, but between . . .
CORTÁZAR

Go to the airport. Go to dream, to think, to wake up or to see ourselves cry. Crying because I'm drinking a Báltica beer and surrounded by a horde of kooks who are all named Vlady, even though none of them can remember who Lenin was. They haven't even read Lenin. They haven't even heard the two syllables of his name pronounced the Russian way: *Lie-nin*.

Besides my stole and my can of Báltica I'm here with my hangover and the tautology of watching the flights arrive from London, Moscow, or Paris. As if Havana itself weren't London, Moscow, or Paris.

Cry in the airports. Cry before the automatic doors of opaque glass and the escalators without their solar-charged batteries. Cry with the customs agents, who open stuffed suitcases from DHL in the name of God, or maybe the World Revolution. Why did I come here today?

The days are tunnels where time cloaks the torments that remain off the clock. I can hear another plane overhead. The roar of an IL-62 or an MIG-15: there are thousands, millions of them; they are flies, *barzuk* bumblebees: this is a country of mammalian aircraft. A similar weightlessness is only experienced by those who live in the airport, like me. The nomads of Stalinophilia and all that *perestroika* shit from the heart. A starting point.

The woman on the loudspeakers bleats out the arrival or departure of the next plane. The volume of her tears is connected to the stateless decibels of my identity and its three Marchenko roots: country, family and profession. How to illuminate myself with all the integrated circuits on the white page of my mind? Which four kinds of debt do I still owe myself before I begin to ascend? Case in point, going on.

When the suitcases come out, one is leaking plumes of *kolokol*. I know. I'm God, I'm Vladimir without Ilyushin-62. I'm a Little World Revolution piloted by fifteen MIGs. This package of plumes is loaded with infinite and infinitesimal wings of *kolokol*, the mute bird of Siberia: the best music is its silence. This suitcase is contraband. It is the Mommy Dearest Russia that wants to emigrate from the New Russia and land here again. Like in the '80s. In the same thermonuclear pressure cooker.

Of course, here in the airport the ocean doesn't exist. Or it's far away, too far to be heard over the loudspeakers. Here everything is glass and formica and metal, and it spills over into the harshness of my sleepless nights, my shelves full of passports with dead permits from CPSU. The airport is a carnival of powerful masks with visas from the USSR; it's the terrain of a rhizomatically post-national logarithm. Case in point, new subject.

That's why it is so important to come here every day. To come. To go to the airport is not only to drink a Báltica, but to see which entrances and exits my faith in faraway family is using to come and go.

After emptying the beer can and playing with my cigarettes, I only have a soft tide remaining: tides of logos, advertising billboards filled with our doctrine. I think about how to clear my head, how to wake up. About dissipating the psyche that moors me with the terminal inertia in my eyes. I cross myself the orthodox way and dare to shed another tear. Ingeniously, pretentiously, or stupidly, I think:

What is it to have a body? What is it to be a body? Who roams around with a candelabra searching for certainty in this country?

Trapped in rhetorical cycles, here in my delirium I know I have to take at least a spark from so much stupidity. Anything. A word, a bad translation. A bolt of lightning against the bluffs of my wails. The bacteriostatic enzymes in my tear glands. To sell offenses or to buy neurons: pain, money, movement, food, silence, objects, thinking, clothing. All mixed together: such is the ideal of the glass rock and the coral stone.

Go to the airport to receive and give imagination (i*mall*gination). Go to repress mental lacunas: the dream that rises and the nightmare that falls in the midst of fatigue and tradition. Case in point, period.

My discourse ends. I hear my name over the loudspeakers. Then a woman calls me by my war pseudonyms in times of peace:

Loxandra Shviétsova . . . ! Vera Marttini . . . ! Ipatria . . . !

Then she sounds out my full Christian name:

Marousha Stanilovska Dagmar Natasha Iliana Romanovitch!

And again she simply calls me:

Orlando Woolf!

Every day her nasal voice follows me here. I am the airport. She is my faith in faraway family. But in the end I never have prosthetic wings or legs for my attempt. And I don't understand either.

No one ever sends me any contraband. Or those customs technicians seize it with their Internet detection dogs. So amid all the hugs and signs and flags and hats, I stand up on the plastic table, scream and jump. Then I abandon the dry can of Báltica and the pack of cigarettes I still haven't opened. And I make a peaceful retreat from the Daddy Dearest International Airport.

3.
Two mirrors illuminate one another.
ZEN SAYING

I stand before the mirror and play with the night's melted wax as my hands dream of a man's muted sperm. Guarding against his sharp snorts in the darkness, his double profile that suddenly increases my bilingual languor. Collapsing symbols, reflection and optical defect. The blurred light of the urban forests, unmeltable wax in the seven arms of the candelabra: cosmic zero, lubricious book, horizontal sheath that begets the desert, virgin vagina, cracked conch. My bedspread is a desiccated ocean and I masturbate in ethyl vomit and blue blood froth. I writhe like a wailing child, a swallow in the arms of the New Man or the Elder Brothers or the Old God. Surviving in no time, without a single reader. It's called angelic writing, and to practice it can be diabolic.

4.
Knowledge of things is acquired through their appearance, but it is the heart that reflects a knowledge of reality.
LIN HSIEH

Before my blood drops and the pigeons take flight, I sink into certain uncertain ideas as if they were worn shoes, or the obstructed valve of an Aeroflot engine. Coagulated void twenty thousand feet in the air.

I feel like a zombie with no argument. No bridges on the way, just tunnels. Bricks from the Berlin Wall are now paperweights in offices. Brave blood turned barren or, even better, the indigestion of vice ministers who eat lobster and drink beer of the Bucanero Max variety. I look at myself. Holes in the soles of my shoes and pouting lips. I endure the pain of a tooth growing in: number twenty-eight (my age). I go on foot, drifting between the Cinemateca and the Muelle de Luz, where a little ferry operated by the State takes me to the other side of the sea.

It's Regla, refuge of the buccaneers. I walk into the church. The altar is terrible, but in the geometry of its *santería* Madonna I see lines plagiarized from the Virgin of Kazán. The houses here have roof tiles and skylights, sur-*dying* monuments from two or three centuries ago. I find the cobblestones on the narrow streets irresistible and brutal.

Get ahold of yourself, I say with each step. *Find the path and love thy neighbor as much as thy poetry, as much as the exile of thine errancies, as much as the unlikely rain that is yet to fall.*

Everything around me spins and weaves into a spider's web underlit by streetlights of Spanish time. The scenography imposes its macabre style, the moribund psychopathology of being colonial. I need my own First World, right here, in Regla, in America. The nonsense of need: I suppose that's my madness.

I turn up the hill toward Colina Lenin, now serving as my local tourist destination. I think about Margarite Yourcenar's worst book: *En pèlerin et en étranger*. I would like to have used that title for my book. I'm always behind. Everything pivots around a quote we don't know, or that we ignore until the time comes for us to die: we are this lacking, this tangentiality. Starting with a lack of energy in the form of money, the only antidote against the repressive poison of family and megaindustrial nets.

Of course, I don't understand a thing because there's nothing to understand.

I reach Blackie's house. I find him cooking over a wood fire, now, in the twenty-first century, almost at the base of the Colina. He hadn't been expecting me. He excuses himself. He looks nervous, as if he thinks I might bite.

The conversation centers around emails, a practically infantile documentary about rock and roll in Cuba, the dangers of watching more than three hours of any 3D channel.

My head throbs like a ten-gigawatt speaker baffle. I ask for some coffee and Blackie takes me to a neighbor who sells it out of his living room. There, a young black man is also sipping out of a plastic cup as he gesticulates ominously and doesn't shut up:

"I did an akinatón, paco, two valerians; I'm checked out and it's been three days since I've heard from myself."

And then:

"Get out of this country! Find an airport! I'm too black to get through, but you, you Russians," he said, pointing to Blackie and me, "Go find an airport and split!"

And then again, on his last sip:

"I'm a metal worker, a son of metal workers, and I'm going to build a fork. Let the Yankees think it's a new kind of national weapon. As long as they leave me in peace. I am me and I don't eat white hens! The Naval Base is infested with sharks and Bush will have to hire people from the Greenpeace party. Make peace, Russians, and free the path to freedom!"

I return my plastic cup without taking a sip of the coffee. It probably tasted of lightning, I imagine, of international politics, woodsmoke, mosquito fumigation, an RNA flavivirus, pumpkin flan made with Spirulina, Polivit and Bio-3.

I say goodbye to Blackie, his neighbor and the young black man, who by now is winding down his preachy broken rhetoric: he sells everything from noodles to IL-62 parts. I think of a satire: *The Erasmus of Folly, or In Praise of Rotterdam*. I think it was written by a Cuban halfway between Reform and Restoration. There's a reason why Havana has been one and one thousand times Rotterdam, capital of amiable universal insanity.

I leave slightly stupefied and walk back down the hill toward the bay. At my back, the crumbling church and a square with bells, cannons and an equestrian statue of some general.

I claim my place in line for the ferry. I'd like now to savor the brackish flavor of strangers. To smell flesh seared in the purifying fires. To inhale a few lungfuls of hashish. To be a strange Barbie, with no friends and no buyer. I hope the stars bleed out onto the bricks left over from the Berlin Wall and splatter all over the pigeon poop. I hope the city opens up and swallows me whole like in a modern soap opera or the worst Piñera poem—along with my worn but still imported shoes.

I disembark again at Muelle de Luz and then realize I hadn't done anything. I hadn't even knelt at Colina Lenin to pray. I had never been there. Maybe everything was a dream too unreal not to be real. I'm a flash of light now.

> 5.
> *Why are we so limited? Is matter part of my consciousness?*
> ROZITCHNER

"Is the roof flying off on us?"

"*Asere*, friend, is the roof falling in?"

"What roof? Who? What is the roof? Of what molecules is it made?"

"They say they're going to sell shingles, *tavarich*."

"French shingles or shingles from Trinidad or French shingles cast in Trinidad?"

"Confiscated shingles. From Regla. From the Colonial Era."

"Transparent shingles. Plastic. From the airport."

"Zinc shingles. Hot. The kind that will sever your head in a cyclone."

> 6.
> *In German, the word "sein" has two meanings:*
> *"to be" and "his."*
> KAFKA

Like someone who wakes up in a mirage of early morning as the bat transforms into a rose and the she-wolf becomes the desert's glare. Like someone squawking upside down in an angiologic cave. Like someone who uses a video camera to rub her clitoris in the foreground, almost breathless. That's how I first open into "lotus pose," and then, more relaxed, into "satellite pigeon pose."

I don't resign myself to masticating nirvanas like some sad lizard. I don't want to see myself in some mirror's inverted contortion. If the country yawns under my pillow, then hate is a boomerang of blame that cuts down my other self in my dreams.

I feel my eyes, like sad chameleon signs, the foreign abyss of a pilgrim so provincial that please. I press the video-camera vagina inward. I hit the REC button. I'm invisible and only on the magnetic tape do I recover my corporality.

Visceral and mental aikido. Images fast-forward through my veins. Antonioni films. Julio Cortázar interpreted badly according to the Rule of Osho. Fortunately I'm not ruled by my period today. Everything is recorded in black and white, high contrast. After a long pause the curtain rises for the final sequence.

J. Cortázar pulls a rabbit out of his sombrero and offers it as a gift to Vlady, who listens to the fragility of the silence through a metaphysical cloud without hemoglobin. Cut. The rabbit is not uterus red, but blue. But it's not a unicorn either, and it lets itself be carried away down the river, and the linear yet somehow pyramidal smoke cleans its coat. Cut.

Julio C. falls and opens a wound like the lance in Christ's side. His blood is red and phosphorescent green and yellow like the cellulose of an old book. Cut. The poor blue rabbit flees into me. Cut. I feel a tickling and open some more. My legs look like the needles of a compass. *Aguardiente*, 180 degrees. I push the camera in up to the wire and still I know I'll give birth. Or abort.

J.C. bites me in the esophagus so I'll shut up. I film him looking wrathful in a big close-up. Cut. Antonioni signs his frames with my pregnant female saliva, with my milk that's white like paper. My mind, too, faints in white. And now mental aikido is impossible. Or maybe too possible.

Julio Cortázar, however, is a sad lizard sleeping out his frustration. I don't shut up, no one can stop me from narrating in images. I'm an incessant state of filmation. I am a one-woman film-nation. Cut.

I hit the REC button again and extract the camera as if it were a baby. Or a fetus. Or a Tampax tampon. Paradoxical how hitting the same key both records and stops recording. Or gestating.

> 7.
> *You must create the task yourself.*
> *There is no disciple in sight.*
> KAFKA

I review my collection of tattoos. Quotes from books, match-burn scars. A magnificently stupid and trivially brilliant reading:

It's a mode of truth: not of truth coherent and central, but of truth angular and splintered. De Quincey.

To be the dark, solitary eye-nerve watcher/of the world's whirling diamond. Kerouac.

What does the essence of technique have to do with unconcealing? Heidegger.

Not with the L of the famous lucidity but with the other L of liberty, of lunacy that illuminates the depths, the lugubrious labyrinth, lambda loca, *lightning bug before the light, long before the first locomotion or logos.* Rojas.

I try to erase my collection of tattoos. Scrape off the quotes with a scalpel, leaving scars from sharpened metal on my skin. It's a stupidly magnificent and brilliantly trivial sanity. Cut. No credits.

ELEVEN STORIES FROM THE NEW CUBA

8.
We're all protagonists,
but in a story without a script.
ROZITCHNER

I clean the camera lenses, defecate and leave for a poetry conference in Zone 999 of Alamar.

I take a pink city bus, a so-called *camello*, on the verge of extinction. The driver lets me in his cabin in exchange for a little flirt. He's a desperate man and, for this reason, immortal. Through the rearview, dirt brown like chocolate, everything spins and blends. Carousel country, Nestle-brand kaleidoscope homeland.

It might not seem so, but this last sentence is a parody of the English soul: the Tower of beheadings, Big Ben, the Hindu spacesuit of the Taj Mahal, the Thamesis of poetic mandalas from the Anglican Church (all of it, of course, through John Lennon's clown glasses or the frigid Lady Di).

The poets regard me with disgust and admiration. They sniff me. They think I'm a performance chameleon, a professional menstruator. I lean into the lens and shout:

"What is it to have a body? What is it to be a body?"

And then, pushing PLAY with one of my nipples, I project the reel in 3D:
"I'm a metal worker, the daughter of metal workers, and I'm going to build a ladle!"

The images follow each other in the 3D viewer. There go my polystyrene organs. Lili doll, Barbie of barbarities. Blue blood. Semen accumulated since the founding of the Russian Empire in capital letters and the Cyrillic consummation of the Little World Revolution. There go veins, artful arteries, super-highways of hepatic music from Liverpool.

I take off all my clothes in public and then put them all back on, without shame. No big deal. No one understands a thing. The screen turns to fuzz and there's a deafening whistle. Scratch. It's just the test pattern. Or that's all people see. Experts call this the "Kalashnikov visual fatigue" effect.

They applaud me. I spit. They throw me out. It's the Britannic phlegm of Alamar. I walk back from Zone 999 until a yellow city bus almost runs me over. The driver calls me *"zuka"* but then invites me into his cabin.

Reality is a circus. It's cyclical. It's a circle. It's a great big zero. There's a reason we're in the two-thousands already: the year zero.

Now it would be spectacular to film a Decalogue that covered all the amusing apathy from the year 2000: it's always the year zero. Now is the time to set aside our narrative imbecility and finally start narrating as if we were illiterate. Now I look over to the driver and his macho Cuban tattoos and, flirting, ask him:

"Who roams around with a candelabra searching for certainty in this country?"

9.
Each instant of life, whether hostile or pleasant,
holds something unique.
Protin

"Peter's chocolate bars and little chocolate eggs! Little chocolate eggs and Peter's chocolate bars!"

"IL-62 mattresses and racks! IL-62 racks and mattresses!"

"Noodles, flavoring, clothespins and foam mops! Foam mops, clothespins, flavoring and noodles!"

"Cake rolls and *polvorones*! *Polvorones* and cake rolls!"

"Lilies and sunflowers! Sunflowers and lilies!"

"Old newspapers and magazines from the USSR! Magazines from the USSR and old newspapers!"

"Empty bottles and cans of Báltica! Cans of Báltica and empty bottles!"

"Passports from the USSR and expired CPSU cards! Expired CPSU cards and USSR passports!"

10.
The man became a sieve,
the Frau had to swim.

PAUL CELAN

The mystery of the formula is insanity. Unaided insanity as a process of starvation, a flux of senile pregnancy: a shock to the cerebellum. The tangible forgetting of the desert and a past litany when eyelids close and we return to ourselves, conscious or almost. I am still me.

No texts pass through my fingers and I no longer feel the naked contortions of death. I'm at the summit of something, on the edge of nothing. The peace of my open sex has me bent over with laughter and smelling heretical, of lymph and sweat. I am still alive.

A terrible sore bleeds worries through my palate. Everything acquires a purple texture, one of desiccated viscera on the verge of rotting: putre*fiction*. I don't go, I don't come: I stay, and my tongue is free amid the countless disasters that have allowed me to resist. It's the glorious calm of a miracle, where I don't even need salvation.

Everything is slang, sophistry. I am completely insane, but I am not me either. We are all insane, but the mystery will always be simply a formula.

Third Eye of the Madman
MICHEL ENCINOSA FÚ

I pull out my cigarettes and light one for Prism.

"I'm going to shred her when I see her," he says, taking a nervous drag.

My feet are killing me. This same old three-hours-late shit. I don't know why I bothered to clean myself up and come running down here. At least I'm getting some air through the holes in my jeans. This black skull shirt, on the other hand, isn't doing much for my thermal equilibrium. Or this hair. It's down to my waist. Fuck it. I'm cutting it soon. Long hair's out around here anyway.

I size up the rest of them. I spot a Metallica T-shirt so hot it might make me come. I'm going to tell my old man to get me a couple, but in white. These Augusts are what they are. Let my old woman wash the shirts. And I'm tired of my rings. Better offload them on my cousin, all ten. Get new ones. But not before I tell Indio I'm ready for him to give me some new tattoos. He's got a weird vibe. Girls and dragons doing it, that kind of shit. In any case, Maya's not here anymore to tell me about how she doesn't like men with tattoos. Repressed egos, marginalized autodidacts, inked-up walking doodles, don't even think about it, she'd say.

Fuckyou is over on the corner cruising some English chicks in full-on jungle mode. Don't ask me what the hell they'd see in Fuckyou, salamander kid in skeezy tribal post-hippy get-up. He was probably born wearing it. I stare at him so hard I don't even have to call his name, and he saunters over smiling from earring to earring with his rotten trap.

"What's happening, Prism?" They shake hands. "What's happening, Email?" He reads my forehead. "You want some?"

Prism throws me a look and I hand over a bill.

"That buys me double today, Fuckyou. It's my birthday."

He stiffens.

"I've told you like twenty times to stop calling me that."

"Fuckyou," Prism gestures with his head, smooth and shiny. "Is La Cabra around?"

"She's with Panga," says the salamander, barely able to contain his delight. "They're already in. Panga's seeing the sound guy."

Prism nods, thinking, and slyly says to Fuckyou:

"Aren't you tight with Panga? At that thing with Joker you and Joroba held Piolín so Panga could break that bottle over him."

"Ok, but Panga was a friend of yours too."

"Was. Piolín's been with me a long time, and he's looking for you."

"Shit, you know how it is. With a piece like Sátira in the mix anyone's prick would blow. Their motherboard too." Fuckyou is on edge; some rasta dude in a crochet hat is chatting up his English chicks.

"Well, that certain someone would leave with their dome spinning and their body more frozen than a cheap beer in a town of paupers," wagers Prism, more solemn than Moses on Sinai. "Every bad weed meets its machete."

"Ok that's enough, leave it in neutral." Fuckyou smiles and opens his hands. "You want more just say the word," he says, and walks away.

I watch him go over to the corner and practically dislocate his neck looking for the English chicks. Then he spots them getting into a tourist taxi with the rasta dude. I get a kick out of it and say so to Prism, who doesn't respond. You can see he's fucking pissed. Don't even try to wrap your head around it. Shit between Prism and La Cabra goes way back to the '80s. So they have a history. Shakespeare is shit. But when you stick your hands in shit they come out dirty, so I don't. Their shit reminds me of my parents. Except Prism is my main man, my brother, my mentor and I won't think twice about getting my hands dirty for him.

"Give me that," he says.

I give it to him.

"Light one."

I light one.

He goes to leave. I follow.

"Where you going, Prism?"

"Over there, Monster."

"Prism! Hey, long time!"

"Hey, Baqueta."

"How's it going?"

"Fuckin' pissed."

"With her?"

"Who else?"

"Shit."

"Hey, you got anything?"

"I got something for everyone. Good stuff."

"Email, shit, I didn't even see you there. Prism's always got swag for his friends. Did you get it from Fuckyou? Piolín is after him."

"Today is going to be good," says Monster.

El Baqueta, who knows something, touches Prism on the back, just above the waist.

"Shit man, our friend here is packing."

"Prism, just chill," Monster advises. "Look, the cops are all up in our spot. They already shut down La Palma, El Pabellón has been closed since that thing with the kid and one of these days they're going to call La Madriguera off limits."

"I don't need anyone to get me in. I can take care of myself," Prism assures us, looking past our heads and out into the night.

Concealing my pride, I slide my hand over the knife in my pocket. New, first time out. I bought it from my cousin the flight attendant. It's not as sick as Prism's AK bayonet, but it cuts just as good.

Monster produces a liter bottle. We drink. Inside they're still running sound tests.

"Prism, don't tell me you're really going to slice her."

"Drop it. He knows what he wants."

People are getting restless. When the fuck is this thing going to start? Now all we need is a blackout like last Saturday. The ultimate boredom. And this is when I start thinking about Maya. But I don't want to. I came out to relax, feel good, turn twenty fucking years old and share whatever comes my way with Prism, my brother. I light a cigarette for him.

"Has anyone seen Fuckyou?"

"Hey Piolín, drop the act. You can't just follow someone around like a ghost. That someone's gonna turn around and put a boot to your head."

"Right *compadre*, someone has a heart after all. And look, don't freak, if this thing gets ugly the cops will shut it down."

"I just want to have him located. I'll take care of the rest. There's no way he'll catch on."

"That's up to you. He's on the corner."

"Thank you. Give me a drink. Prism, La Cabra is already inside."

"They told me."

"Ok, bye then."

"Wake up guys, they're selling tickets."

"Email, let's take some of this stuff now in case the cops show up later."

Down the hatch. And who gives a shit if I'm pushing my limits? I turn twenty fucking years old today.

We advance in a snaking single file of frowning chain links. Then we find our spot next to the speakers so we can hear it good and loud. This place is packed with hot bitches, so I'd better kill anything I feel for Maya with one stone and try not to leave here alone.

They're putting on some recorded music, which they blast. Alice in Chains: "I'm the man in a box . . ." Maya's kind of thing, of course. The discharge of pseudointellectuals who think they're something just because they've read Joyce and Castaneda. Generation X. Does it really exist? "Oh, oh, oh Jesus Christ . . ." The pre-cyberdelic liturgy. Do they really exist? What a shitty bunch. And where does that leave me? Generation Z? Or XXX? Do I really exist? I'm feeling it now, I'm feeling it. Good thing. Truth is this concert isn't really my style. I like it harder. Electric black metal, drills through a wire, sadomasochistic vampirism and satanic genocide. Die faggot.

Prism is a straining periscope, showing off his teeth to the five horizons. Now he tenses up, groans and freezes.

"Don't be so obvious," El Baqueta prods him. "She'll catch on and you won't be able to get near her."

The live guitar finally breaks. Porno para Ricardo opens. I don't know who the fuck Ricardo is.

"Ay Manuel, I know you'd give your ass for a steak . . . Ay, Manuel . . ." Blessed is censorship. Or ignorance.

Someone knocks on my head with their knuckles and I spin around ready to fight:

"What the fuck?! Rusa, beautiful, what's happening?"

La Rusa plants a kiss on my lips:

"Come here."

She lets me back her into a corner and put my hands all over her. The slut. Such a slut. She must have gotten into it with her parents again and needs a place to sleep. Fine by me. She knows me well, my weaknesses, my quirks, so it won't get complicated. It's my birthday and I'm not about to take the trouble to show the ropes to a total stranger. I bring my fingers to my nose:

"You smell like you always do. And you shaved."

"You want me to suck you off right now?"

She doesn't know how to restrain herself, so you have to know how to manage her:

"Hold out for a minute, baby, calm down."

"What the fuck is your problem?" She shoves me in the chest. "You don't like me anymore?"

"Do you always have to be embarrassing yourself?"

"Look who's talking. I'm not the one who vomits after two sips."

"And I'm not the one who spent a night in jail after the police caught me fingering myself at La Rampa."

"It was *Interview with the Vampire*! Brad Pitt and Tom Cruise! How could I not?"

"Eat shit." I sprinkle her with a few kisses and we leave it there. Do I know her or what? Then suddenly she stiffens. I look, and Prism is standing behind me.

I light his cigarette and he leaves. La Rusa exhales:

"Jesus, what a presence."

No wonder. Back when she was with Prism he really laid down the law. He's strict with his women, even if they're only with him for a day, and when he hits them it's always with his fist, just because. I smile:

"That's love. You miss him, huh?"

"Die," she says, and tries to knee me in the balls. "Don't even go there, faggot, you know you're the one for me."

Of course I am. Prism with his shitty little room in Old Havana, a gray sheet and two changes of clothes. Me with my VHS Panasonic, air conditioning and a pimped-out Aiwa in my room. Of course I'm the one for her. Life is hard. She still wears the earrings I gave her last December, from the first time Maya and I broke up.

"I got a new tattoo from Indio," she confesses. "Look . . . "

Keep talking, slut, keep talking. My prick is about to explode and you're just the one who's going to help me bring it down again.

Back home, in my drawer, I have the fifty dollars my old man gave me so I could buy myself whatever I wanted. La Rusa loves beer. And I'm sure she hasn't eaten anything. We're going to go all out tonight. Spend at least twenty. She's not worth it, but I am. I'm about to say "Let's get out of here," but that's when a hardcore fight breaks out right next to us, and someone lands an elbow in my ear. I'm ready to react, but she grabs my arm:

"Email, please. Leave it and let's go."

I swallow my pride and follow her a few steps.

"Besides," she adds, "you only wish you had the balls. A little shit like you couldn't even . . ."

"Hey, who is the slut here?"

"Ay, my child, even that weird Maya chick was the one playing you when you were together."

I kick her once in the ass and again in the knee. She tumbles. I throw myself on top of her and we exchange a few swipes. She buries her boot heel in my gut. *Dyke, whore.* Then I stop: it's not worth it. I don't even bother to look at her as I walk back to the hardcore.

Who did she think she was? Calling my Maya a "weird chick." My Maya. My dyke, my whore, my bitch Maya. I want to see her so bad. But no. When they dump you, you have to keep your head up and take a deep breath. Don't be a loser. Don't let it get you down. Today is my birthday. I don't want to think about Maya. I don't have the energy. I'm done. Another round like that and I'll lose my high, and that's not going to work. I need to refuel. Down the hatch. That's more like it.

The hardcore is going in full force. A legion of urban samurais on a collective suicide mission. They pounce, wail, kick and body-check at random. And right in the middle of it I see Fuckyou, the frenetic salamander, woozy and sweating buckets.

Someone climbs onto the stage. It's Piolín. He's going to dive. Head first. Go figure. He falls right on top of Fuckyou. Tremendous confusion. Piolín gets up and scampers on all fours into the tangle of legs. Fuckyou gropes at his back, gropes it again, and grimaces. I strain my neck looking for Prism and the rest of them. Piolín comes up to me:

"Did you see, Email? Did you see how I crushed him?"

"I think you're the one who got crushed, brother."

"Blessed be those who missed it, and fucked," he laughs, and then shows me a safety pin. "My friend who works at the HIV Clinic gave it to me. Good, right my friend? So, so good, *asere*—ay!"

He's pricked his own finger playing with the pin.

"Ouch! Shitshitshit." He drops the pin, inspects his finger, pulls a crazy face, picks up the pin, looks my way and comes at me.

Not happening. I palm his face, give it a shove and fire off in the other direction like a fart laced with gasoline. I don't fuck with that shit. Ay, mamá. That killed my high. My balls must be this small. I'm about to shit my pants, I've gone all weak. Imagine if he had decided to act like a beast and got me . . . And when that shit goes down you really don't have any friends. When that shit goes down all you want to do is drag Mohammed along with you. At least Piolín didn't follow me. Where are all my friends? I just hope that burnout doesn't think to jump me from behind.

Far into the crowd I spot Panga with La Cabra. A rush of inspiration tells me to follow them, and after two seconds I bump into Prism.

"Hey, Prism."

He doesn't even look at me. He cuts through the crowd and I follow in the empty trail behind him. He finally stops, and I plant myself in front of him:

"Prism, old man!"

"What do you want?" He still won't look at me.

I light a cigarette. But I don't even get the chance to inhale before he snatches it from my mouth. I snap my fingers in front of his face:

"Prism, my brother, look, if you see Piolín, word to the wise, friend . . ."

"Friends are as good as shit," he says, giving me a blank stare. "There's no such thing as friends in this place." And he walks past, nearly knocking me over.

To hell with him. Him and his issues. A man can only drown in a puddle with a woman if he wants to. And all I want to do now is get out of here, crawl through Maya's bedroom window like I used to do and talk to her. About I don't even know what. Whatever. And if she wants to kick me out, call her parents, I'll just latch on to a leg of the bed so hard not even a sledgehammer could get me out of there.

"Heyhey! What's happening?"

I prick up my ears. There's trouble near the loudspeakers. A head, smooth and shiny, sinks into a sea of arms. Shit, that's my brother. *Hey, excuse me, shit. I'm coming through, dammit. Get out of the way.* There are like ten people fighting each other. Panga, Piolín, Monster, Fuckyou, El Baqueta, Prism and I don't even know who else. La Cabra is on the floor, under all of them, getting kicked. Prism drops his bayonet. Panga tries to retrieve it. I go in.

Fuckyou is the first to have me by the neck. Don't fuck with me. I whip out my knife. Someone else jumps me. They're biting my leg. I don't understand a thing. I have my face against the floor and there are three guys on top of me. They're so heavy. They don't even notice me. La Cabra looks at me, shrieks and begins to scratch at my face. All I can do is spit in her eyes to stop her from taking mine out. I manage to turn over, throwing my elbows and knees. My knife gets stuck in something. My hand suddenly goes hot. I pull, but I can't get it out. The bodies turn, everyone screams, I let go of the knife, get up and run, shoving everyone out of my path. I don't stop until I reach the barbed wire fence, which I grip, climb and jump. Then I run and run, a million miles per hour down the avenue, and the harder I run the harder I cry.

I don't even stop to catch my breath. I just slow to a trot. I synchronize my breathing with my stride. Tomorrow I'll be behind bars, just wait. I should have left with La Rusa. I'd be able to run and run for a hundred years if it meant I wouldn't have a cop at my door tomorrow. I have a terabyte of empty space in my head. The wings of the serpent, the scales of the tiger, the third eye of the madman.

And I suddenly realize it feels good to run. Look, maybe everything will be fine. Let them guess who did it. No one knew I had a knife, and no one would have seen it in that mess. Pity. It was new. First time out. And what a time it was. The blood on my hand has dried. I rub it off. I hope I didn't kill anyone. It felt like a thigh. I had the impression it was a thigh. I'm sure it will be fine. Why wouldn't it be fine? Things like this happen every day and they end up fine. I try to smoke a cigarette on the run. I can't. And I don't want to stop. I throw out the cigarette before I even light it. Then I keep running.

I run past a café. The people inside look at me as if, well, you can imagine. I pretend not to care, but really I just want to explode. Why the fuck do they always have to look at me like that? Even worse, at the stoplight, I hear a boy ask after me with the old cliché: "Mamá, is that a man or a woman?"

Now I'm coasting downhill. I let gravity do the work. My socks must have holes in them by now. These boots are shot. My toenails are pressing into my toes. I need to cut them. Listen, I can't do this anymore. I spot a broken bench, a blown bench, a chipping, blessed bench, waiting just for me. Aw, shit.

"Ismael."

I look up. Open my eyes. Close them. Open them.

"Maya. What's up?"

The dude with her is dressed like he just walked out of Carlos III, and he eyes me jealously as he hugs her close around the waist:

"Come on, let's go get some cigarettes on the corner."

"You go," she says. "I'll catch up."

The dude throws me another look and walks away.

"Nice guy," I say to Maya. "I don't know what he has that I don't."

"He doesn't write me poems with spelling mistakes, for one." She sits down next to me and looks me in the eye.

It's obvious he doesn't write her poems. I take out my cigarettes. We light up.

"So you're getting married tomorrow."

"Yeah. Five o'clock in the Vedado. You can come if you want."

"Maybe I will. Where's the reception?"

"At his house. A shit ton of bottles. A cake this big. You should see my dress."

"Long?"

"White. Gorgeous."

"If you were marrying me I'd have you in a miniskirt and black leather."

"Yeah, but I'm not marrying you."

The dude comes back, pulling out a Monterrey. He watches her smoking, sucks in the last of his cigarette and flicks it away.

"I'm going." She stands up and slides back into her high heels. "Come tomorrow. Will you come?"

"Drop dead." I stare at my knees to avoid looking at her face. "Just drop dead. Both of you."

They leave. So do I. After twenty turns through streets I don't even know, I finally arrive back home. Prism, Panga and La Rusa are waiting for me at the door:

"Panga saw you with the knife. They say you almost took out La Cabra's liver."

"Who says?"

"As of now, him, Prism and me. But what are friends for? Don't worry, she won't die. They'll close it, sew her up and that will be the end of it. Good thing you left. They really grilled us."

"And hey, just so you know, we're going to Peñas Blancas tomorrow, and we're totally broke."

I walk inside, go to my room, walk back outside and hand them the fifty dollars. Prism pulls my knife out of his pocket.

"And you don't even thank me," he tuts, then nods toward La Rusa. "Ask her where she hid this during the pat-down."

"I can imagine."

They leave. La Rusa stays: "I won't bother you?"

"As long as you don't bother me."

I let her go first into my room. It's already two in the morning. Yesterday I turned twenty. She lies face up, then pulls down her skirt and underpants.

"I need you to see if I hurt myself with that little knife of yours."

I lean over and slide two fingers inside of her. She's wet, very wet, but she's fine.

"You're fine," I say. Then I pull out my fingers, take off my clothes and walk into the bathroom.

Thirty Seconds of Western Silence
LIA VILLARES

(home time)

My mother paused in front of the door to the balcony and said, "look how pretty my Flamboyant is getting," as if she didn't remember that her Flamboyant had been pulled out by its roots just a few months before.

(—me time)

Dust. So much dust. I breathe it all the time. I wipe it up and do nothing but wipe it up, partly so it can fall again over the piano and books, covering everything over and over, entering the lungs to later be exhaled and so as always. *Somebody new, someone to love. Tus peines sur mon coeur et vos pieds sur une chaise.*

There is a tear in the painting. It almost reaches the wall, and then I lose my sight, vertiginously. There's no one and nothing to look at for that matter, but still. My eyes. I'm falling asleep. Though I keep myself awake. Drowsy, I'm dying for sleep. Marks on my body. Each time I bathe I discover new marks: scratches on my buttocks, scabs I constantly tear off that bleed so much, bruises caused by surprise blows from things I failed to notice, which seem untrue and provoke from me all manner of questions, doubts, indifference and, lastly, despair. They sadden me.

Mosquitos. Every day I fill this room with light yet they remain, thirsty, flattened under my loud palm, useless. Trains. The trains again. The buses, the cars, the lost footsteps of the people in the street at night, late. But mostly the trains. The trains that never stop running at the worst times during the sleepless night, make up part of the night, of everything, like a slow watch, like the radio and its program *Jazz Corner*, insipid appointment for those keeping a late-night vigil. Like my progressive blindness over pages of Kerouac under so little light. Like the light from my sister's yellow lamp in the next room, like her voice in a pure whisper sometimes.

Articulate the words to disarticulate the sense, all meaning, implicit or not, in each one. The late-night vigil. The emptiness of all moments without. Inanity. Though not knowing who, in the end. Though not waiting, or wanting to see. Haste. Delay. Hope. Anxiety. Tranquility. Finitudes. One day so much time deliciously squandered and the next unattainable. Need, acceptance, indecision, conformity. Numeration. Obsessions. Unsalvageability. Certainty, memory, inaction. Vagueness. Artifice. Mistakes. The open decay in everything, under all lights. Under the roof or the tree. Lounging, reading, gloating, dissatisfaction, narcissism, loss, music. Crystals entangled in the strings of a broken wind chime. Eyelids opening and closing. Continuously. Coltrane spitting out incoherent phrases, incomplete, interrupted. Fragmentation.

The entrance of the piano and the applause at the sax. Paralysis. Movement. Stillness. Significance. Depiction. Non-history, non-action, non-narrativity. Zigzagging or walking in a straight line. Or in circles, walking toward, up to, the house. My house. The radio. (Ah, and last, don't forget, please don't ever forget: guard your smile.) Worse weather, worse face. Despondency and more dust. *Quelqu'un.* Ink. Miles Davis. Morricone. Patience, late nights, sterility, strangeness. Calluses on my feet. The urge to urinate, the strong urge to brush my teeth, to hear someone whisper my name, always the same urges. Lime torn from the walls. Immobility. Thirst. Verticality. Relief. Noises. Darkness.

Drops falling, bugs, fear, cats, eyes, kisses, the softness of the moonlight, alcohol dribbled on the floor, meows, screams, cries, the wood in my mother's nearby door creaking. Her constant sighs. Repetition. *Ad infinitum.* Sameness.

([n]o-me-time)

I think my hands have shrunk. Or at least my left pinky finger has become infinitely miniscule, so now it seems to have a single and fragile phalange.

Starting from the beginning is the absurd, before the absurd: to go from the absurd to a greater absurd.

Chronology is fake, all succession of events is fake and distorted like those governed by chronology. History is chaos.

So any story can start anywhere, insignificant. Even less important is the path traveled, where it starts or how to map it.

In this way, as I try to bend my tiny phalange, my lips mouth the lyrics to a Brazilian song that now seems sad, but perhaps is happy, naïve, hopeful. Heaped against the fully covered walls, disarticulated fragments of memories—fragments of disarticulated memories—each with its own mute history. Semi-present fragments, inconfessable to eyes prying and innocent.

So much what-do-I-know contained, frozen fragments, dead-living memories, passive macabre zombies, in the walls like fossils of butterflies or lightning bugs, phantasmal fractals of sleeping time, in the gathers of crumpled paper, behind frames with or without glass, broken, hidden, displayed without the least amount of fear.

People's perverse, sick custom, repugnant and sadistic, of conserving everything, of wanting to be close to their unarticulated memories, materialized in ink and yellow. Musty witnesses, schizoid and cruel evidence of time. The morbid mania of simply wanting to remember, continuously, to retain lost moments, to be scandalized by the terrifying notion of the sole existence of the present time, wanting to re/turn to past time, to rip off the healing scab.

The absurd rejects suicide to remain between the confrontation of human interrogation and the silence of the world. Lies. I think I dreamed my hands were shrinking, growing ridiculously tiny. I wanted to sleep for a while. It's as if I can only be near you. Again.

But to spend most of the time sleeping in lies is too abhorrent, it's another society subjected to order, equally asleep. Though it doesn't worry me too much. Hardly at all.

It's impossible to start from the beginning. And not very functional. To persist in the idea of absolute sadness is chronic, says Bataille. The recognition of failure, indifferent out of uselessness, waste. (Cruel? You feel light for my overwhelming bewilderment.)

Chortles, a startled face, twisted in pain, the anguish of hysterical laughter, the extreme condition of drowning in a cry, absurd, assured, impure. I don't know how to tell you about my pain, I don't know. You just have to jump out of bed with the firm conviction of having shrunken hands.

(night time)

The smell of Refino rum perspired on urban transport at midnight, the smell of saliva and Popular cigarettes. The guy didn't stop looking at me and looking at me and saying things like: "Nothing went by here?" or "Do you have a light, beautiful?"

I had Henry Miller to read, under the scant cold light from the two tubes at the stop. The light was insufficient and inappropriate, but it let me keep my distance from the one guy and relate, alone, to the other. Only us, and a few delinquents looking to make the night on dark and gloomy corners in decadent Luyanó. Henry wanted to assassinate a few of them, exterminate them all while he still had a chance, before it was too late and the cancer had spread all over the planet. The main problem was getting out of America, in every way.

Sometimes his descriptions coincide with my reality, like now. The sun would rise and still there would be no disgusting, mortuary bus. The alcohol-infused sweat was the worst—after the bad breath.

I sat a little closer to the light, farther from the guy. The fabric of his shirt was worn through, dirty. I tried to read page after page without looking up to see if something was coming. There wasn't much traffic. An ambulance stopped at the hospital and two men unloaded a stretcher. Then a silent patrol car drove around the block a few times. Nothing more, nothing less, nothing.

After thirty minutes the first *guagua* passed; not mine, so I sat down again, disgusted, and opened the book to a random page. The guy was still there: it wasn't his bus, either. We were waiting for the same one. With an eastern, solipsistic patience. He sat with his head between his knees, his legs outstretched, respecting the distance between us.

I silently expressed my relief and read a strange and delirious fluid of words, heaped one on top of the other and not at all resembling the typically restrained and happily economical tact of North American prose. As a continuation of this hysterical lapse, the stupid *guagua* finally came.

I sighed, relieved, and put the book away. I managed to sit in the darkest seat, losing the guy near the middle of the bus, among spaces occupied mostly by adolescents, detached like half-awake dummies.

(empty time)

You can't write on a full stomach, or an empty one. You can't write if you're tired, or too awake. Or sad, or relieved, or satisfied. If something hurts, you have to let it pass. If you rush it, slow down. And if you can't find a way, wait a while.

When you find you're scaring yourself, you're already a failure. Try to remain and, if it's not in your plans to submerge yourself because you don't want to, at least float on the surface; something is better than nothing. If you can't eat with your throat so closed, lick the palms of your hands and toss your hair a little. Always wear something clean and cover your body with moisturizing cream. Prepare the best breakfast for yourself and memorize all the sunrises you can, with all their sounds.

If it is very hot, take off your clothes, walk barefoot, jump rope, make the best fruit smoothies. If you are consumed by the urge to play chess, go visit your father from time to time. Drink lots of water if your hangover is enduring and strong. Eliminate as much as possible all unnecessary yawns, all accumulated boredom. Write to your friends, it's not that hard. Go over everything you have left to do, even if it disgusts you. Clean the mirrors. Go to the movies at least three times a week. Invent pretexts for not staying at home, unless it's to read or do something creative. Make sure your feet don't get too dirty when you walk in the street.

Listen to all the music you can. Keep reading, collect as many samples as possible. Always go to sleep when you need it, especially on government holidays. Distance yourself from anything labeled national, as a measure against profound irritation. Pet all cats that will let you. Remind anyone who is camera-shy that the Native Americans believed cameras would steal their souls.

Escape sunburn in the afternoon. Soften your hands. If you're hungry or thirsty, stick out your tongue and lick. Yes, in jest, eat and drink what you want, but don't strain. Remember that even in times of drought the land still keeps its color. Do not ignore too much. And if you know a lot, don't torture yourself, don't kill yourself to kill time because only your death awaits you. Either way, remember where you are, still, breathing dust.

(empty time)

My best time is when I'm doing nothing. When I don't have to do a thing. And this even includes making plans. Work is the greatest evil. It goes against natural desire. Carpius knows it.

My room is a personal map, a map of myself, like a body, or a town in ruins. Sometimes it's too old, with forgotten highways and unnamed cities, dangerously invariable. It makes me sad sometimes. The house, while more ramshackle, is more resistant. I've also set about learning not to wait, either, for anything. Under no circumstances. Too many permitted pleasures are ephemeral, untamed, adorable. Excessive in their short duration. As almost always, and at the price of limited freedom, chaos is attracted in a surprising way, well-received, clear, like a new order, a hateful word.

Over the paper lamp, I made a tree and filled it with miniature boats, also made of paper. Opaque. Almost invisible. I love them. They'll never sail any sea, not even a paper one.

This room is a time machine. A museum piece. I should charge admission or lock myself in forever. Every now and then, every few days of never trying to calculate a thing—not even to look for patterns—I feel an urgent need to cut myself off from the outside. To detoxify myself from all the noise and smoke and sun. And especially people. Though here inside I've taken great care to eliminate as much as possible any light coming through the cracks, which let enough in to accent things in the shadows, to give them some color. But noise is a complicated case in this city. It surges like a drill, motor, loud talker, bicycle bell, whistle, happy or hysterical shouting, or both. Grates, cans, horns, trains. An orchestra. Of people. Like a drunk in broad daylight it's my late night, just below my balcony, improvising a bolero with a bottle and some impressive cries; next to Maurice, it would be hard to tell who is more minimal and masterly in his use of resources. At least Pink Floyd, at a sufficient volume, is enough to sooth me in the mornings, when I try to go back to sleep.

It's thundering. Incredible that it's going to rain. *How wonderful*, Carpius would say. *Water.*

(thirty seconds of western silence)

Shagai: Astralagus (anklebone). The convex sides of the bone are opposite the concave sides. A game that consists of throwing a sheep's anklebone into the air, in which a winning toss lands on the convex sides, called horse and sheep; a losing toss lands on the concave sides, called goat and camel; and any other toss doesn't count.

Does it have any ink? Very little.

The day sneaks up on me like a leper. Miller says God isn't dead. There is still osmosis somewhere. Still. Some articulation. And then again this being with oneself. These mutisms. This being pursued.

Twice more, Gottfried Benn: Woman-light-brown reels toward man-dark-brown. Hold me, dear; I'm falling. I'm so weary at the neck...

So you know, I'm also living dog days. I'm another hour of water.

In the afternoons, my eyelids stir like woods and sky. Drinking tea, eating rice. My time arrives in a baker's suit after being up all night on a double shift. Tactile organ, no. Are you a happy person, are you sad now? Are you a sad person, are you happy now?

Like spirals of dust or dispersed ashes, ideas don't leave a trace of their trace. A passing torrent, a salt storm in the desert. I'll make an igloo of the petals at the ancient hour, a brilliance that never blinds me less. Contemporary sterile lethargy, I grant myself thirty seconds of western silence.

Nothing to do, nothing to see, in my headphones Charly is what's happening. (Only silence presides over silence.)

Someone approaches and slowly says to be reasonable, because my ears are small and I have to tell them sensible things. *I'm not your labyrinth, whore!* I shout, swatting her away. Impertinent fly.

The chair suspends me in the nothingness for a fraction of time frozen on a flour-covered apron. They shoot and in the photo I'm me at four and a half, sitting on a sepia tricycle. Smiling at a sepia void. Ahead, a trolleybus. The streets of Santiago. Alleyways. Two ridiculous scooters hide my ears.

The extinction of double perception. It's *The Movie*, by Beckett: Put out the animals, conceal the mirror, cover the furniture, take down the prints, rip up the photographs. To be is to be perceived, to exist is to allow oneself to be perceived?

I let the coming and going balance me, once again suspend me, twice again, more, and the balance comes and goes and comes and goes. Back. Forth. Back. May it never st-st-stop. Bumbling. I fiddle again. More ideas. What's scary is my perception of myself through myself. In-sup-press-able.

Disarticulated Bayamo Boulevard, marbled granite sun. Ultra-violent sun. In spite of the cold and fictional Bayamo, a Bayamo for the Bayamians, run. I collect random samples and when my exhaustion grows I stop. I go to sleep, I grant myself thirty seconds of western silence.

I sleep on national holidays as a measure against profound irritation of my scalp, my sensitive epidermis. I sleep a lot, long. I reject any efforts toward production. Then I take my camera and convince the photophobes in the sepia of their ancestral backwardness; in the end I tell them sensible things. In the end, the preservation of their souls is as insignificant as their faces degraded in the silver and gelatin.

I soften my hands, hydrate my body with Agua de la Tierra, registered trademark. I lick my hands and toss my hair; I lick my cat's paws that are hanging over the fruit bowl and run my hand up its bluish back. For breakfast we have a Sunday televised infantile abortion with blaring music.

The deterioration and creaking of a city—I write in red ink on the door to my balcony—correspond to the deterioration and creaking of its people. It's impossible to keep—I keep writing—the lurid exterior from rubbing against the interior. Someone approaches and slowly says I have pessimist tendencies toward the negative. I silently smile.

Be reasonable, Adriana; they ask me what the hell do I want to do, seriously. I can't just go around so generationally disoriented, so tired and lethargic, with my sterility and my propensity for meditation, contemplation, and masturbation. (Drinking tea, eating rice.)

Lugging the hours of wagered days, Lezama was clear when he said that in Havana we had grown used to playing the years and winning their loss.

Enough. I'm not your labyrinth, get lost with the days, erase yourself from history, my silent smile means I don't want to do anything, absolutely seriously. I am what is happening. I want to play until my bones waste away, until I dislodge my soul and send it to hell. Anything but knowing where I am, still, breathing dust for air. Anything but this morning disgust, this mild disgust for burnt coffee and tar in my lungs. Inside and outside, the skreaking. Inside and outside. The skreaking. Case in dust.

In order to arrive to the absurd in the midst of the death and routine reserved for a dismantled city, you must eliminate all sensitivity: sensitivity is hope. I lower the volume of my radio, I rise up with the firm conviction of having shrunken hands.

Juan Piñera passes in front of me. He's on his usual nighttime wander through the Vedado. I run to give him one of my little personalized cards with a quote from his Uncle Virgil: "I sustain nothing. Nothing sustains me. Our great sadness is having no sadnesses." His lips twist into a smile and he nods. And I wait for him to reveal some mystery or fascinating secret in return, hidden in his impenetrable gaze of master sorcerer, alchemist of unexpected melodies.

But no, nighttime phantom insomniac marauder like me, he only gives me an unsettling look with his penetrating eyes, dark and tired, and I feel stupid with my two braids under my hat that covers my little ears and helps to distance the noise-music of the Street.

He only tells me to take care, that I should be careful this time of night, and says goodbye, after indicating which bus I should take to get to the outskirts, where I happen to be going at the least convenient hour possible. I stick out my tongue at him and then run, farther than I wanted, until I lose consciousness.

In its baker's costume time insists on pursuing me. Bumbling. It sneaks up on me like a leper. Is there any osmosis left over there, anywhere? Miller's voice slows down. Any articulation? I suspend a final moment in the nothing. Still.

You have to put out the animals, conceal the mirror, cover the furniture, take down the prints, rip up the photographs. The echo of my voice grows distorted. My body abandoned to the enormity of the atomic accident, to the accident of the atomic enormity, to the atomic enormity of the accident . . .

I am permitted to grant myself thirty more seconds. Of western. Silence.

That Zombie Belongs to Fidel!
ERICK J. MOTA

There's a red-and-black sign at the end of the alley. Cracks in the wall and a few exposed bricks are visible from the house. The asphalt street, crumbling from age and neglect, boasts old potholes from its moderately glorious past. Plants spring forth from their confines and onto the sidewalk. All is peaceful in the neighborhood.

A figure walks slowly along the asphalt, a few meters from the house. It's headed for the main street, three blocks away, where the P2 and the 174, the only lines that run through the neighborhood, stop. It moves silently, awkwardly, dragging its feet. Its gestures are almost comical. Sometimes it lobs its head back and forth, looking for balance. Sometimes it seems drunk, unable to control its body and on the verge of toppling over onto the sidewalk. It's not an oversized child, nor is it a hopeless alcoholic. Its skin is wrinkled and rotting. Sun-scorched sores cover its face and arms. Coagulated blood encrusts open wounds. Only an idiot would fail to see it is a zombie.

How strange to see it alone, out on the street in broad daylight. They always used to be escorted by someone. There were checkpoints everywhere. If the police saw someone with a zombie, they'd stop them right then and there. They'd ask for their ID card and the zombie's documents. If they didn't have the right permits, the zombie would be confiscated. Sometimes the police would even take the owner down to the station. Unauthorized zombie possession, I think, was the charge. It used to be that wild zombies would only roam at night. Those were the people who had been bitten by their own zombies and transformed. Hence the night patrols. An entire police unit had been dedicated to the problem.

Since then things have relaxed, as they always do. The police only request the escort's ID card. At night they patrol less and less. The days have passed more slowly since the Z virus first appeared. Zombies now roam freely through the streets and no one fears them. Everything will always be the same in this country: a mess.

"I think there are even more zombies in the streets now," I say aloud, leaving the window.

"Don't even think about talking to the neighbors about the zombies again," Panchito says from his bedroom door. "Remember what happened during the last Committee meeting."

"You're right."

Panchito was right. I shouldn't have opened my mouth at that last Committee meeting. All because I need to know everything. Or, as Mamá would say, to show everyone I know everything. I spoke about the zombies during the meeting. The whole neighborhood was there. No one was more qualified to discuss the topic than I was. I'm the only one in the neighborhood who works at the Center for the Investigation and Development of Zombies.

In short, I tried to explain CIDZ's efforts to develop a vaccine against the Z virus. I informed them that the correct pronunciation of zombie was in fact *zombí*, according to Haitian Creole. I told them the story of Bokor, the dark wizard who revived the dead to form a zombie sugarcane brigade, using them as slaves to work the fields. Until the dead's relatives recognized their loved ones, whom they thought had been buried. They went after the dark wizard for what he had done, and returned their loved ones to their tombs. The problems began as soon as my story ended. It was as if no one had understood a thing. The chairman of the Committee stood up and glared at me with murderous eyes.

"Wait just a minute, *compadre*. Are you claiming our country is governed by a dark wizard who has enslaved the living dead?"

"You wait just a minute, I said nothing of the sort..."

"Everyone knows the Z virus was created by the CIA to attack Third World countries. Things may have gotten out of control up there in the USA. But like the *Comandante* said, we turned the disaster into a victory. Now the zombies are a weapon of the Revolution. Sure, we use them to harvest sugarcane, but they're not slaves—they're zombies of the revolution!"

"But if I..."

"We refuse to be destabilized by enemy hogwash..."

And he kept speaking. And speaking. Or should I say insulting me. And invoking clichés about the Revolution, socialism and zombies. I first tried to explain that the very use of zombies in the sugarcane fields, or in the May 1st parades, was possible thanks to a serum developed by CIDZ, which allowed the primary reflexes of the living dead to develop slowly, suppressing their uncontrollable urge to eat. Thus allowing the zombies to obey certain simple orders.

In vain. They didn't understand a thing. Then I tried to backpedal a little. I said it had nothing to do with the Haitian legend. That the Revolution's intention was right in trying to assimilate the zombie problem dialectically. It was only a legend, after all.

The chairman didn't understand that either. He just stood there with his arms crossed and said:

"Besides, everyone knows in Haiti they speak patois."

I didn't have anything more to say.

Well, there was one more thing: *I'll shit in your mother's cunt, you fat racist.* But back home the TV was broken, and we still needed them to give us our Panda TV so we could keep grandma entertained.

Another thing. Everyone in the neighborhood knew Panchito wasn't a zombie. I had gotten a certificate for him from CIDZ and he hadn't bathed in three months. From far away he looked like one of them, but it was all a ruse so he could be eligible for the ground beef ration reserved for family units that included a zombie.

So I took the conversation to be over. I bit my tongue while the fatty with the mustache continued to offend me in public. Those of us born with above-average intelligence quickly learn to keep our mouths shut.

Since then I've hardly left the house. Nor have I seen the chairman of the Committee. He hasn't set foot outside for days, not even to take out the trash. I know he's at home, because I can see him walking around inside his house. But he doesn't even appear in the front door.

"Panchito, be honest"—I try to change the subject—"don't you miss bathing?"

"Sometimes, in the summer. But now that winter's coming . . . though I never liked water much anyway. You know that."

"I sure do. I remember how you used to scream in the bathtub. Mamá would get so mad!"

"Now at least you guys can benefit from my terrible hygiene. I used to have to hear it from our old woman all the time. 'Look at your brother. He's got a job at CIDZ and you sit around all day doing nothing. They're going to throw you in jail.' And on top of it I had to bathe. At least now she doesn't hassle me."

"Well, I'm the one who is about to go out and play dominoes. I'm so bored!"

"Don't be so sure. There are fewer people playing out on the corner every day. Most of them look like zombies, but they're not. You can tell because their flesh isn't rotting and their eyes aren't all white. But they have a lost look in their eyes and they move funny.

I went down there the other day and there were a ton of people around the table. Timba was there, and Pancha's son . . . what's his name? Omarito! They were all dead silent. A silence of the tombs, my brother. Since when have you seen a game of dominoes where no one speaks?"

"Wasn't dominoes invented by monks who had taken a vow of silence?"

"But that's not how we play in Cuba! We shout, my brother! But that's how it is. Zombies are in style. Even kids these days want to look like the living dead."

"No way."

"Seriously! Not me, though. I do it for the ground beef ration. And to get the section chief off my back. But some kids, the ones who sit in the park on G Street . . ."

"Where the freaks hang out?"

"Exactly. They make themselves up to look like zombies. All they do is walk back and forth in silence from Calle 23 to the Malecón. Then the police come and order them to go home. No one puts up a fight. They all board the 2 a.m. bus without a word. The P2 passes by here packed with freaks and emos. All silent. So silent you can hear yourself breathe. Like in a tomb."

"It's not that bad."

"It is! I'd rather stay in."

Out in the dining room, grandma is still watching her new Panda TV. New out of the box. Mamá is cooking something in the back. And I kill some time by reading the newspaper. *Granma* is the only paper we get. Red letters in strange type spell out the word for *abuela* in English. Underneath, in white letters against a black background, it says: *Official Publication of the Cuban Communist Party.*

For all the years I've read *Granma* I've never gotten tired of that part. As if the line were some wondrous and exciting thing. As if it might transform from night into day. As if one morning it might say, in red letters: *Official Publication of the Cuban Republican Party.* Or maybe, *Official Publication of the Christian Democratic Party.*

I read the headline: *ZOMBIES, WEAPONS OF THE REVOLUTION.*

I don't even bother with the rest. I know it's a crock of shit. Like everything in *Granma.* I put the paper down. I have no clue what to do. And there's nothing to do in particular. I'm bored.

I'm used to waking up every day at five, wedging myself into two different buses crammed with people, and working for eight hours. I don't know how to do anything else. It's what I've done my whole life. First at the Biotech Institute, then at Tropical Medicine, and finally at CIDZ.

When the accident happened they sent all the researchers home at sixty percent pay. *A bio-leak*, they told us. But the standard time period for quarantines had passed. No one had called, no one from the Institute had come for me. Strange. Our bosses always work us hard, and never give us more time off than they have to. Something big must have happened at CIDZ. Something to justify this kind of silence.

They used to pester me all day. Any irregularity in zombie behavior and they'd call. If I refused to come, they'd say I had been issued a phone so they could locate me. But now the phone doesn't ring. No more calls at three in the morning, or cars from the Institute parked in front of my house.

I thought about calling. Asking them. Sometimes I fear the nature of this mysterious bio-leak. I'm afraid it got away from them. What other bio-products could escape from an Institute like CIDZ besides zombies? What kind of zombies could wreak such havoc?

I won't call. Over the years I've learned: never volunteer. If they don't want to call, better for me. I can still get my money every month from the ATM. I don't need to do volunteer work. And I could use the rest. At least that's what I thought in the beginning. Now I'm dying to do something. Even something useless. I'm bored out of my mind. I still wake up at five in the morning. Every day. Religiously. Even though I have nowhere to go.

There's a knock at the door. Mamá yells "co-ming," and Panchito runs to his room to start playing zombie. It's one of the mosquito men. Officially known as an inspector in the war against *Aedes aegypti*. Their mission, on minimum wage, is to contain a possible dengue epidemic on the island. But no one calls them by their official name. Everyone says "the mosquito men." The mosquito men don't care what people call them. They only care whether you have any uncovered stagnant water.

This guy is really weird. Too quiet. But his skin is in good shape. He walks gingerly but not with the clumsiness of a zombie. He's human. Or at least living. I've spent enough time with zombies to know.

"Do you have any water tanks?" he asks in a voice that's flat, like an answering machine.

"Two, one on the roof and another in the basement."

Mamá is standing in front of him holding her inspection log, a document whose purpose I've never figured out, despite my Master's degree in biochemistry.

"Do you have any spiritual vessels?"

"No."

There's something strange about this guy. Each time he asks a question he looks as if he's about to write down the answer, but then he doesn't. He asks all the usual questions. The same questions they've been asking since they declared "war" against mosquitoes. This, instead of acknowledging the imminent danger of a dengue epidemic. We've always been good at inventing enemies for ourselves. Still, there is something different about this guy. He asks all the right questions in a flat monotone. This might be normal. These aren't exactly charismatic types. But when we answer, he poises the pen as if to write, but then doesn't write a thing.

He doesn't even pretend to write; he simply doesn't. As if writing were some ancient, abstract memory buried in his subconscious.

Strange. Very strange. Especially since I've seen this kind of incomplete motor-function cycle before. I've observed it too often at work to miss it now. A typical reaction in our trial subjects. Zombies. But this guy doesn't look like one. He can even speak. Though I haven't yet heard him utter a complete sentence.

"Do you have any flowers in water?" he asks.

"That depends on the flowers," I say, interrupting the conversation, despite Mamá's severe look.

I know what I'm doing. If I'm right, he won't be able to respond to this kind of statement. I hope with all my heart that I'm wrong. As for Mamá, she isn't amused in the least by my intervention.

"What do you mean by that, Rafael? Can't you see our comrade is in a hurry?"

The sentence freezes in midair. Our comrade inspector for the campaign against mosquitoes has just lurched in my direction like a predator. White eyes and mouth agape, he roars a little as he advances with a vacant look.

"Panchito, get Mamá out of here!" I shout.

In a single leap my brother springs from his room, clasps Mamá by the shoulders and hustles her out of the zombie's reach. Panchito was always quite fast when he needed to be. He's not as lazy as everyone thinks. Meanwhile, I've escaped from the zombie's path. I kick it in the calf. I don't even need to kick hard. Zombies don't have great balance. Security at CIDZ kicks them all the time. Its body falls heavily to the floor.

We have to act fast. Everyone's life is in danger. Just one bite, one trace of saliva and we'll have a new zombie in the family. Then it will only be a matter of time until there is no more family.

"Hold it down, quick!" I yell to Panchito. "Don't let it get up!"

Mamá screams hysterically. Panchito and I each hold it down by a shoulder, in a fruitless attempt to immobilize it. The zombie grunts. Its strength is immensely superior to ours. Little by little it staggers to its feet, despite our efforts, winning the battle against the force of gravity. It's only a matter of time. Mamá is still screaming.

But Grandma is quiet. The TV is still on, even though no one sits in front of our most recent import from the People's Republic of China. Grandma was always the practical one in the family. Without a sound, she has left her beloved armchair and begun to move slowly (at her age there's no point in moving quickly) toward her room. She reappears just as the zombie is nearly standing. We are still hanging from its shoulders in an effort to weigh it down, barely able to restrain its leaden movements. The song from Cuba TV National News drifts in from the dining room. The zombie still hasn't bitten anyone.

Grandma is carrying a heavy old cane. That terrible one Grandpa used to use, may he rest in peace. Cedar with a silver handle. It inspired such terror in the neighborhood hoodlums that time they thought they were robbing a poor defenseless old man. A souvenir from back when things used to come from the United States instead of Russia or China.

Mamá finally stops screaming. The zombie groans. Grandma delivers a hollow-sounding blow. Coagulated blood splatters against the floor and walls. The bones in its head make a crunching sound as they break. Grandma freezes, the cane raised high. She looks like a samurai from an Akira Kurosawa movie.

The zombie, on the floor, is no longer groaning or moving.

"Close the door!" Mamá regains control of the situation. Panchito rushes to carry out her orders. "Rafael, you work with zombies. What's all this about living dead that can speak?"

Not only can it speak. It can also look you in the eye, and its skin isn't rotting off. Even if its blood is still coagulated. I hate it when everyone looks at me expecting a convincing explanation. I carefully study the body and its collapsed skull. I inspect its skin. I try the reflexes on its limbs, which are still moving, like a dead lizard's tail.

This simply can't be. It violates the principle of entropy, it violates I don't even know how many laws of physics. Smooth skin with no signs of deterioration isn't consistent with the progression of the Z virus. Or its focused eyes, almost like a human's. It could even say simple sentences.

"It's evolution," I say aloud. But in reality I only speak to release some of the horror mounting in my mind. "They're adapting to us. They've learned how to mimic."

"What do you mean they're adapting?" Panchito is practically hysterical. "Like they're evolving? How can they evolve if they aren't anything to begin with? They're zombies. Living dead. That's it."

"It's not the zombies, it's the virus."

Explaining this to the family isn't much use. They wouldn't understand. Zombies are something more than living dead. They're biosystems. Reservoirs for the only form of life we haven't found a way to eradicate: viruses. No one is exactly sure whether they are living entities or organic machines. We know how to exterminate faster and stronger predators, but we haven't been able to destroy the tiniest adversaries, like the flu strain. Or HIV.

Now the Z virus is a step ahead of the rest. It seizes control of our bodies, kills them, rearranges the DNA and converts bodies into biting machines. So the Z virus can spread among humans. And now it's adapting.

"It's all our fault," I say. And then a terrible silence falls over everyone—a sign they're actually paying attention. "Our serum helped them adapt to us."

The serum. It had been the serum all along. We failed to create a vaccine. The Z virus was five times more antigenically variable than the common cold. We decided to change the virus's ecosystem. The zombie itself. We wanted to create a less voracious, more manageable zombie. Like in the legend of the Haitian Bokor. Friendly zombies, easy to order around. Revolutionary zombies.

We changed their brain chemistry so they could develop vital functions, like smell, sight and touch. The serum was successful in mitigating their uncontrollable appetites, present in all specimens from North America, Europe and Japan. We thought, in short, that we could bring them under our control.

"We were wrong. We wanted to use them as slaves and ended up giving the Z virus the tools to adapt itself to us."

"But why? Why would it want to adapt to us?"

"It's common for animals to try to look like their predators. That's how they manage to survive."

"Us? Zombie predators? Now you've lost it, my brother. Don't you watch the news? Everyone around the world runs from zombies because they'll eat you alive! They're our predators!?"

"We shoot at them with exploding bullets, we gas them and set them on fire with flamethrowers. And we lock them up in places like CIDZ to use them as guinea pigs. We're their greatest threat, believe it or not. And the serum enabled them to look like us. I have to go back to CIDZ. I have to tell them. We have to take a look at these samples . . ."

"No one is going anywhere!" says Mamá.

Her face looks serious. Everyone is paralyzed by her voice. Like when we were little and she yelled at us. It's not a joke, a plea or an appeal. It's an order. And this is Mamá we're talking about. There's no way around her.

Grandma is back in her armchair, looking at us without saying a word.

"Especially not you, Rafael. We have no idea what happened at CIDZ. We don't know a thing about this mysterious bio-leak."

"But, Mamá," Panchito replies, "we have to do something, tell someone."

"Who are you going to tell? The chairman of the Committee? He doesn't even show his face in the neighborhood. The police? They just roam the streets all day asking for IDs and giving them back without saying a thing. All your neighborhood friends? They can't even pull off any of their old pranks anymore. Even the old ladies have stopped coming around to tell me about the lives and miracles of everyone and everything. Kids don't throw rocks anymore. No one protests. This block is like a tomb. A tomb where the cadavers don't even know they're dead. Nowadays anyone could be a zombie."

There's nothing more to say. She's right.

•

Three months have passed since the attack. We no longer bathe. We only go out to run errands and pick up Panchito's meat ration at the butcher's. Our movements are slow. Our words, monosyllabic. Just like the grocer, the butcher, the police and the neighborhood hooligans. They're all zombies now. Or they pretend to be zombies just to survive. Like we do.

We never open the door. Not for the "mosquito men," not for the exterminators and not even for the police—supposing they ever came. At night we sleep with the windows locked and all the doors barricaded. Not even the dogs bark at night anymore.

Panchito says things must be working somewhere. Otherwise there wouldn't be electricity, gas or running water. Maybe he's right, and someone really is trying to contain the epidemic. I for one don't think so. Things have always worked the same way in this country: out of inertia and sheer miracle.

The zombie bodies at the power stations or the water plants remember the functions they carried out when they were living. They pretend to be human beings, mechanically performing their duties like always. I suppose one day there will be failures too complex for them to resolve. And then darkness will come. And hunger. But it wouldn't be the first time.

Grandma can't unglue herself from the Panda. She always liked to watch it, but now she's obsessed with finding a face that doesn't look like a robot. The anchors repeat the same old news about imperialism, our sister nation of Venezuela and the Five Heroes. All speak in the same monotone voice as the Public Health inspector who was here three months ago.

Grandma insists the people *up there* don't know a thing about this silent invasion. She thinks that's why they haven't done anything about it. "But as soon as Fidel finds out he'll let those zombies have it . . ." she says, clutching the remote and compulsively flipping through the channels.

According to Panchito, all the people *up there* must be zombies too. The directors, the generals, the Council of State, the ministers—everyone. That's why they say Fidel is ill. He can't give speeches that last more than an hour because he's a zombie.

As for Mamá, she blames it all on the Americans. "They'll end up dropping the atom bomb on us like they always wanted," she says. "They'll use the virus as an excuse, now that we're all zombies."

I don't think it matters if the higher-ups are dead or not. Everyone benefits from the zombies. They don't mind working overtime, they don't balk at the overflowing buses, they don't demand to be paid in dollars, they don't write dissident blogs, they don't stage riots. In the end, in some way, this country has always been made of zombies. At least it has always operated as if it were. We invented the mechanism, and now we accept it. The Z virus, along with the CIDZ serum, merely created people who were suitable for surviving here.

The North Americans? The United Nations? The World Health Organization? They gave up on us a long time ago, long before the first zombie. They just watch our news and assume things are going ok. We don't have shootings, or states of emergencies. Everyone just acts happy in front of the cameras, and they always meet the goals established by the Party.

There's Grandma watching the December 2nd parade. One after another, the living dead march with their camouflage, Kalashnikovs, and Vilma laser pointers. They don't tire, they don't sweat, they don't fall out of step. They're as perfect as Hitler's troops.

Too perfect for such a chaotic island in the middle of the tropics. We Cubans have never done anything with such precision. One might say this Zombie Period is our moment of glory.

There, under the gallery with all the generals' gleaming stars, just in front of the gigantic statue of Martí, a white sign with big red letters spells out what destiny has in store for us:

UNITED WITH THE ZOMBIES FOR THE DEVELOPMENT OF SOCIALISM.

Dancing Days
RAÚL FLORES

Hunger for everything I've never had, for everything I'll never have. Hunger.

A lazy afternoon for going home and trying to be alone, an afternoon to somehow spend in this seventies atmosphere that surrounds us like smoke. Like water through the veins in our hearts.

On stage the band is singing. *American woman, get away from me.*

We dance. It's the end of the world, our personal holocaust, it's Café Cantante and the band is the Kents and they're churning out these melodies again with the silky strength of an electric guitar. *I don't know how I got here. I really don't,* I think.

The last thing I remember is someone's house, dust by the window, Nicole Kidman's leopard eyes asking names of the silence. I remember empty streets, lonely people, trees strung with lights and the July sun, piercing my eyelids with its unbearable glare. After that I forget.

I probably came with a bunch of freaks, frayed pants and stony drunken eyes, and then let myself spend my last ten pesos for the month on the cover. Or even better, maybe La Flaca blindfolded me and dragged me here. Only God knows, and God might not exist today.

What I do know is now I'm in and the effects of the drug are dust in the wind, like that Kansas song. Up there the band has changed its tune and now it's "All Right Now" by the Frees, entering our sacred chameleon ears without permission.

We dance. Again and again. End of the century, dawn of a new millennium, destruction of industrial capitalism, philosophical angst over Marxist theories. We celebrate everything and nothing at once. Love rites. La Flaca comes over, squeezing her way through the crowd.

"I didn't know you were here," she shouts.

So I didn't come with her after all, I guess.

"Well now you know," I say. "You don't have to know everything."

All right now, baby, it's all right now.

"Did you bring anything in?" she asks.

The Kents stop playing. "New Year's Day" by U2 blares from the speakers. *Nothing changes on New Year's Day and I will be with you again.*

The crowd, dressed in black and white, gathers under the red ceiling to tear up the dance floor. We dance.

The power of electric guitars, of steel sizzling under fingernails in the darkness. Meanwhile, La Flaca tells me everything here is in dollars and they screen people at the door.

"No one here has any rum and I'm dying of thirst," she says. "Dying. Are you sure you didn't bring anything in?"

Then she asks if I want to take a break. Sit down at one of the tables. I know she's going to ask if I have any money. I also know I'll say I don't.

We make a move for the tables. To see if one is free, by some divine miracle. The Beatles take over the room, *it's been a hard day's night and I've been working like a dog.* And this will be a hard day's night for you, me and La Flaca if we can't find anyone who will buy us a drink. I'm not really very thirsty, but I know I will be in a while. And the girl at my side is a hawk in heat, a wilderness of nuts and liquid miseries in the middle of Nowhere.

Fortunately, God exists today. An empty table and Adrian the German in the corner. I don't know Adrian that well myself, but in times like these we're all as brotherly, humanly and internationalist as could be. (*Arise ye workers from your slumbers/The Internationale unites the human race.*) I know Adrian studies biophysics and hangs out with Carlos and Junior. I know he likes rock, and I also know he has money and that for today—and just for today—he is the solution to our problem. We say hello.

"Are you really German?" La Flaca inquires.

"From Berlin," Adrian answers.

La Flaca looks amazed, as if she's never seen a German before in her life. Then she asks him his name, even though he already told her.

"Like that song from The Calling," she says, when she learns it again.

Adrian smiles. I don't think he's ever heard of The Calling.

"And you, what's your name?" he asks her.

"Jeanette," La Flaca replies.

We sit. "Start Me Up" by the Rolling Stones over the speakers. Adrian goes to get beers.

"I need you to do me a favor," says Jeanette, drumming on the table to the rhythm of the song. "Tomorrow is my birthday."

I want to ask her how old she'll be, but instead I'm thinking about all those books they'll never write about me once I'm gone. All those songs they'll never sing. So many songs. So many. I can't think about anything else. Books and songs. That's it.

"I'm turning twenty-four. Thanks for asking."

I look at her. She keeps drumming to the rhythm of the song.

"I didn't ask."

"That's what I'm saying. You're always so kind."

"And you're as subtle as Snow White. What's the favor?"

"I don't want to make it to tomorrow," she says.

"What?"

"I have a gun back at the house," she shouts over disco music. "It's my dad's. I've even written the suicide note. You won't get in trouble and it would really help me out. All you have to do is pull the trigger. I don't have the nerve to do it myself."

For now I don't know what to think. It's like I'm suddenly in one of those Raúl Flores stories that's full of nothing but suicide and '60s music.

"Have you lost your mind?" I ask her.

Then she tells me she doesn't want to watch her body age. She wants to be Marilyn Monroe, she wants to be Janis Joplin, dying famous, ending it on a weekend. Like Nico, in the candlelight at his funeral. Girl in white in a silver-finished casket.

"Life has nothing left to offer me. How will I fill all the time I have left? Alcohol? Pills? I don't know how to do anything else."

"You could try to study something."

"No," she says. "I don't want anything to do with school. I'd rather die."

The German reappears holding three beers. Cold beers. And La Flaca temporarily forgets all her talk about death by suicide and begins a conversation about things I'm sure she's never heard anyone speak about in her life. International aid, the war in Bosnia, the Berlin Wall, Third World living conditions, World Cup tournaments.

The loud music (Bad Company), La Flaca's clipped accent and her erratic way of directing the conversation all mean that Adrian's preferred phrase of the evening is *no entiendo*. When Adrian says *no entiendo*, La Flaca just shrugs and says, "Forget it. New subject."

In seven minutes they've already burned through eleven different topics. La Flaca is a beast when it comes to changing the subject. She is. But I get tired fast.

"I'm going to dance," I say, when the Kents come back on stage.

"We're coming with you." Adrian is itching to escape his corner.

The guy behind the guitar plays the unmistakable riff from "Smoke on the Water." The kid behind him in the dark glasses poses with the microphone in his best Ian Gillan stance and sings. We dance as he strangles his own throat, searching for the spirit of what's already gone. LP *Machine Head*, 1973, back when they still made real music. Wanting it, wanting something. And we dance.

"Smoke on the Water" and "Fortunate Son" and "Whole Lotta Love" and "Come Together" and "Heartache Tonight." We'll dance to anything. We're an unstoppable machine of youth and adrenaline, trapped in a time that isn't our own but from which—somehow or other—we've never managed to escape. A tribute to lost time, a light show, amber violet, nuclear disarmament.

"Will you do it?" La Flaca asks me.

"Of course I won't do it. Who the hell do you think I am? Arnold the Terminator?"

"Then I'm leaving," she says. "I'm sick of this. Thanks for nothing."

She kisses us and walks away. Vanishing into the crowd, her silhouette fades into the smoke of an afternoon's worth of cigarettes. Nicotine and marijuana for Jeanette, who has abandoned us. A love ballad for her marquise tits and her Turkish star eyes. The Kents tear into their personal version of the classic Iron Butterfly theme "In-A-Gadda-Da-Vida," and we use the eighteen minutes to rest.

"Do you want another beer?" Adrian asks.

We go get beers. The darkness envelops us like ghosts from a past time. The smoke gets in our eyes and will probably make us cry at some point, but definitely not now. There's a time for tears, but this isn't it.

We go back to the table with a few cans. Adrian says "This is so good," and I feel as if I were in another country. New York, Studio 54; Paris, Moulin Rouge. Somewhere else. I don't know where and I don't care.

"All we need now is a little weed or dust," I say, maybe for the sake of saying something. I haven't had anything for a while, and the withdrawal is churning through my veins, and I think I need something to bring myself up again.

"What kind of stuff do you Cubans do?" the German asks. His eyes have an Aryan look to them.

"Anything," I shrug.

Adrian pulls out his wallet and extracts a little transparent envelope. He places it on the table.

"This is what I do in Germany," he says, cutting two lines of pink powder.

Then he takes out a twenty-dollar bill and rolls it. He hands it to me. I use it to inhale and give it back. At first I can't feel a thing, but about five seconds later it's as if a motorcycle is speeding around a circuit in my heart. A song blowing out my senses, seven moons piercing my eyes, three clock hands turning back the lost hours and recycled minutes.

"Dude, what is this?"

"Don't ask," he says. "Do you feel good?"

"Better than ever." Adrian puts it all away. We finish our beers as the Kents up on stage finish their song. To close, they play their rendition of "Show Me the Way" by Peter Frampton, and that's it for them, at least for this Sunday. Prerecorded music pours through the speakers again, Bon Jovi with "Lay Your Hands on Me." And now La Flaca is back. She couldn't get out because they padlocked the door, and in the end she didn't really want to leave as much as she thought.

"Let's go," I say. "This is wrapping up."

"Go where?" Adrian asks.

"Anywhere. To celebrate Jeanette's birthday."

Adrian looks surprised. "It's your birthday?" "Twenty-four tomorrow," she says, unenthusiastically, glaring at me with laser eyes.

"That's great."

Great. Happy everyone, happy birthdays, leaves in the wind, dust in our senses, and everything's fine. The German cuts a line for Jeanette. "A birthday present," he says. Jeanette wants him to give her the twenty-dollar bill, too, but it looks like that's not going to happen.

And that's us. With more lines in us than a math notebook, twenty-somethings waiting for some miracle, hanging out like high school kids. Full of lines and loving our highs. Motorcycles in our chests, songs in our hearts, full moons in our quartz eyes. Full of lines and loving our highs. That's it.

"I'm going to dance," La Flaca shouts. "Are you coming?"

We all go together and let loose dancing to old rock 'n' roll. Lynyrd Skynyrd leads into The Sweet with "Little Willy," "You Really Got Me" by the Kinks, then "Don't Bring Me Down" by ELO, "Slow Ride," "The Boys Are Back in Town," "I Was Made for Loving You," and finally, for a golden ending, the Beatles again with "Birthday." Pure *White Album*, psychedelic, unforgettable. Then it's all over, and they usher us out.

We spill into the street and outside the sun hasn't even gone down yet, it seems. The light grows unbearable, and I don't know if it's because of the chemicals running through my veins or because no god in the sky could stand that much light.

"What should we do now?"

There's not much to do on a day like this. Feel like it's a Monday in the middle of a Sunday afternoon. Nothing can get any worse than yesterday. Sunday afternoon.

One day I'll be able to look up at the sun without blinking, but today it looks like that's not going to happen. Today is the kind of day when God appears in flashes, and our only answer is the strength in our eyes. To look God right in the eye and ask for another divine intervention. Sunday afternoon. It's always Sunday afternoon.

"Let's go to my house," says La Flaca, and we follow.

We cross streets that are empty after an afternoon rain and finally arrive.

"What do you have for us?" I ask.

"Whatever," she says, "put on some music." And I decide on Pink Floyd, a super-depressing vibe for an evening, a mega-depressing vibe for a Sunday, but that's how I feel so I'll just go ahead and admit it. We listen to Pink Floyd, *The Wall*.

So ya thought ya might like to go to the show
to feel the warm thrill of confusion

"Do you have to play that now?"

I think so, but it's not worth trying to explain myself. It's a matter of intuition. It's not you. It's me. It's all of us. Primitive collectiveness.

Tell me is something eluding you, sunshine?
Is this not what you expected to see?
If you'd like to find out what's behind these cold eyes
you'll just have to claw your way through the disguise

Pink Floyd, "In the Flesh." La Flaca comes back with some water for us. "I thought you might be thirsty," she says. "I was dying of thirst," she says. We thank her.

If you should go skating on the thin ice of modern life
dragging behind you the silent reproach
of a million tear-stained eyes
don't be surprised when a crack in the ice
appears under your feet

"It feels terrible," she mutters. "Twenty-four years."

Adrian listens to her. I know what comes next—I've already heard it. She recites the same speech as before and ends with the same request. Adrian listens and at no point does he say *no entiendo*, not even once. He seems to understand very well this time.

"I don't want to make it to twenty-four," says La Flaca, and goes to her room.

You slip out of your depth and out of your mind
with your fear flowing out behind you
as you claw the thin ice

Pink Floyd, "The Thin Ice." She comes back with a six-shot revolver.

"Will you help me?" she asks Adrian.

"Why me?" asks the German, wide-eyed.

"Well," says Jeanette, "this one here doesn't want to and you look indifferent. With all those people you guys killed in the war, what difference is one more little Cuban?"

The German takes the gun. He examines it, though this can't be the first time he's held one. He turns it over in his hands. Then he aims it at Jeanette's head.

"Wait!" she yells. "Give me one more line first."

Adrian obligingly retrieves his little envelope and cuts three lines. For him, for me and for the girl with the suicide bent. We inhale. "Ok, go ahead," says La Flaca, squeezing her eyes shut.

Adrian raises the gun to Jeanette's head and, assuming his best neo-Nazi stance, pulls the trigger. There should have been an explosion of blood, bone and encephalic matter from the other side of Jeanette's head, but all we hear is the metallic click of the trigger and the hollow sound of a non-existent bullet being discharged.

We're speechless. La Flaca opens her eyes. I can see the ghost of a tear in one.

"What happened?" she asks.

Adrian shrugs.

"It's not loaded," he says, in his icy Berliner voice.

"It's not loaded," she mutters. "It's not loaded."

She covers her eyes. I suppose she's crying, though I'm not one to know. I only imagine.

"It's not loaded!" she shouts, then laughs.

She's crying and laughing at the same time now. She jumps up. "Turn this stuff off," she says, "enough Pink Floyd. Let's play something we can dance to. Put on Nirvana, Pearl Jam, Offspring, Garbage, whatever, whatever you want. Anything but Pink Floyd."

Jeanette wants to dance.

"And your twenty-fourth birthday? Are you going to celebrate?"

"I want to live to ninety-seven!" she shouts. "I want to dance! Put on something happy, dammit!"

Then she says to us: "Guys, you can't imagine how it feels. You have to try it. It's better than dust, better than an orgasm, it'll have your pulse racing at 220. It will.

"Thank God it wasn't loaded," she says, relieved, and goes over to the neighbor's to ask for some rum.

Adrian has been staring out into space the whole time, a smile frozen in his eyes.

"Would you have done it?" I ask him.

He doesn't answer. He only opens his left hand and shows me what's in it: six new nickel-plated bullets. Six shiny leaden deaths.

"The question is whether or not she would have," he says, after a pause.

I don't say anything. And when La Flaca returns with half a bottle of wine, I don't say anything to her either. *Things are whatever people want them to be*, I think. There are moments for experiencing the silence, for feeling the cold of the night envelop your footsteps, but these moments pass and no one remembers them. Absolutely no one.

So we sit in a circle and listen to Pearl Jam. We sniff up what's left of the dust and mix it with wine. It all tastes of glory. And we dance. Like puppets hanging from a billboard. Like crystal *duendes* in the window of a general store. Our souls abandon us and we dance.

Eternally.

With the strength of the gods. With the fury in our leopard eyes. And I think we could make it to the moon just dancing. To the dark side of the moon.

Nothing can stop us, I think. Nothing. Do you hear me? Nothing.

That's why we dance. Until dawn. And then we dance a little more.

The Man, the Wolf and the New Woods
ORLANDO LUIS PARDO LAZO

> *I was going to tell you, David, but I didn't want you to find out too soon. I'm leaving." The way Diego said I'm leaving had a terrible connotation. It meant he was abandoning the country forever, that he was erasing himself from its memory and it from his and that, regardless of his intentions, he was assuming the role of traitor.*
> The Wolf, the Woods and the New Man
> SENEL PAZ

1.

I didn't want to go back to Cuba. I didn't give a damn about what became of that imitation of a country. I didn't want to hear another word about it, not even in emails. No news, no chat jokes. No harboring illusions for a change that would never come in the streets, much less in people's hearts, even after the Polish Pope had pleaded for it in the middle of the Plaza de la Revolución. No blogs about the uninspired counterrevolution between embassies and arrestees. No collecting signatures for petitions to force-feed the latest prisoner on hunger strike if the Northern Empire didn't liberate the hero spies. No Cuba. Understand that first of all.

I didn't have any family left there. At most a few ex-lovers cauterized as ex-friends. I hadn't heard a peep out of Germán, for example, since the last century and millennium. Much less from David. And as for Nancy, I had the feeling it was best not to know.

Nor did I feel the need to look after anyone there. Broad and alien is exile. Life is elsewhere. My Cuba couldn't be something else I lacked after twenty years without a Cuba. Twenty years spent so far from H—, that provincial city whose middle-class pretensions came second only to its revolutionary ones: *Our Habanada which art under the heavens...*

I always shivered at those naïve theories about nostalgia. I had adapted to having no past. Then earlier this year, just as I was getting used to it, I found myself at the Cuban consulate in Washington, applying for my former Cuban papers. Lengthy, expensive procedures, in which I participated not without reluctance, and with some nerve, given all the anti-Cuba writing I had published in sundry newspapers. I handed over my cash with no guarantees in return, knowing I would never reclaim the least of my rights.

Maybe that's why I didn't get caught up in any of it. And in the end I was finally issued a Cuban passport again, in spite of my "enemy citizenship." A passport that came with a flaming "Permission to Enter" the island on page three, as if I needed a visa to enter my own country.

I lost count of how many "how have you beens" I sent out in PDF. But even worse was that my email (notstrawberryorchocolate@gmail.com) ended up on a mailing list for triumphant news about our country, propaganda sent eight days a week by diplomats at the consulate. Soon enough, though, and almost without realizing it, I had purchased a ticket and boarded the plane.

Acute heartache from Cuba we suffer..., I once wrote in one of my "experimental *décimas*," a product of so much sterile success. Now I read those lines as wordplay by an immigrant intent on winning over the journals of our so-called intellectual exile. And then came the Yankee scholars to conceptualize, at a conference, that mine was "Cuban poetry from the late-century diaspora," and then my name began to appear in poorly-translated anthologies. But I'm the only one who still remembers those little asymmetric verses now, at this timeless time, as they open the belly of this flying piece of junk made by Cubana de Aviación and request permission to land. To acubanize.

The noise is deafening. Touchdown on the runway makes me want to vomit. How marvelous, how menacing, how mediocre: miracles with a small *m*, as a small flight attendant helps me to unclasp my seatbelt, giggling the way *mulatas* always do.

I didn't want to go back to Cuba, dammit.

But dammit, Cuba wanted me back.

And for the first time in this new century and millennium I breathe the creole air under an enormous picture of Fidel, defining from on high the now fifty-year-old Revolution: *change everything that must be changed ... the meaning of this historic moment ... never by lying or violating our ethical principles* ... and a preposterous etcetera.

It's possible I had already wiped Fidel's features from my mind: how his index finger always seems to point right at your temple from any angle, his oppressive speech. For an instant I thought I might have died in flight and, as punishment, was about to be revived in the middle of an endemic version of *Lost*, but twenty years in the past. 2011-1991. RIP. *Rev. in Peace.*

"Welcome to the capital of all Cubans," spits a black man, who is magnificent despite his nylon uniform that lends him the gloomy air of a monk from the Cuban Ministry of the Interior. He sweats. I sweat. We sweat. Grammar sans apartheid. I am here now, I blink, there's no way back. The nightmare is just an awakening.

"Thanks, compatriot," I smile sarcastically and am suddenly overcome with the fear that I might not have landed in Cuba after all, that I'm pretending all over again, starting with the language. And as I drag my suitcase toward the revolving EXIT, a single phrase bores into my brain: "Jesus, Diego, what's with this charade of going back to your old country?"

2.

Repatriating Lezama Lima's unpublished handwritten works was only an excuse. I had smuggled them out of the country two decades before after buying them for one hundred dollars from a famous functionary (he's still alive, so I can't name him), along with the last letters Calvert Casey wrote, before his suicide, to a Cuban Lord in London.

The beginning of the nineties in Cuba was atrocious. We were all accomplices to corruption, to the sale of objects and souls. Socialism or marketing: *We'll sell . . . !*

I preferred to ignore the rest of that decadent decade. It was painful enough to distance myself from everything without letting myself feel the pain. To leave everything, everyone. Germán's talent for selfishness. Nancy and her conniving candor, her periodic self-abandonment in bouts of depression caused by the men who would use her for sex and leave. Paranoid Bruno, so manipulative and arriviste, so repressed and brutish behind the hetero guise of his communist closet. Ismael's intelligence: technically, his counterintelligence. And David, a total break. My Diego's David lost forever. The David Álvarez dreamed up by Diego in 1991 so he wouldn't die from the horror of the Special Period.

In fact, only one of the unpublished works was indeed unpublished. The rest of the "originals" had been published in the *Journal of the National Library*. But this particular work really was unpublished. Unprecedented. The definitive UNPUBLISHED WORK of José Lezama Lima and probably of all insular literature, not counting the pages that had been stolen from José Martí's *Campaign Diary* and Ché Guevara's *Bolivian Diary*.

In my power, on a page torn from a notebook belonging to the Republican Department of Accounting and Finance, under the Úcar y García letterhead, in the Maestro's unmistakable handwriting, pulsed the lost poem from the posthumous novel *Oppiano Licario*: in prose, not verse, as one would expect. Three line-bursts barely as long as their pompous title: *Summula/never suffused/ with morphological exceptions*. With no danger of anyone suspecting it might be of value, I had slid it past customs agents and into Cuba without incident, tucked among my letters from relatives; just as I had sneaked it out of Cuba thanks to a Czech diplomat's bag in another December—in 1991—around the time when pieces of the Berlin Wall were becoming souvenirs for socialist bureaucrats-cum-mafiosos or, at least, managers.

And so I brought it with me into the main hall of the National Library, which practically borders the Plaza de la Revolución to the right. I planned to claim I was magnanimously "donating" it, that I had come across it "by chance" at a lending library in New York. And that would be that. Case closed. Guilt banished. The repentance of a worm who wants to go to heaven even though he dies knowing he'll never become a butterfly. And just before, I don't know, asking to see the director to give him the Good News, curiosity led me to the cafeteria bathroom, down in the basement of that building I had come to know so well when I was young.

The mournful atmosphere hit me as soon as I opened the door. It was so different from the luxurious hunting grounds it had been during my student years. Lustful. Where you could sit for hours and be stalked by a nice macho reader, the kind of thing Cortázar would have loved. Where you could let yourself be surprised by how many militants would unzip their flies for the first man who knelt at their feet, hum a combat hymn, stare up at the false ceiling and pretend to piss until they climaxed with the most silent orgasms of the Revolution. Where you could, in short, slake your thirst for semen between the Ministry of the Interior and the Armed Forces, free of charge. I used to call this sure thing "barbed love," "freedom in a minefield," "broken dam," allegories like that. A debauchery as prodigious as it was prohibited, a divine gift in all the despotism, delirious desires that no Gay Pride parade or statue in New York had ever been able to beat.

The place looked so sterile now. The neon lights either blinking or blown. It smelled of shit, literally: the garbage cans overflowed with newspapers. No more genitalia graffiti or telephone numbers scribbled in pencil on the walls. No water in the original nickel taps. No air conditioning either, though there was a catechetical black woman perched on a panoptic stool, indiscreetly making sure no one peed on the granite floors, and for the service of watching you empty your bladder she asked for coins, preferably not in Cuban pesos.

Humiliated, I fled from that Hades of scientific materialism. I struggled up the stairs of tarnished dignity, and it wasn't until I finally reached the Reading Room that I recognized my error. The key was in the elementary-school quality of the wall that dominated the room: ephemeris, herbal medicine tips, activities for the month, an attendance and punctuality record, milestones to be met by the departments, magazine clippings, marker lines, verses from Apostle Martí and an anthropological etcetera. My Lezama Lima didn't deserve to be abandoned in a dreary place like this.

The library was like a dead nightclub, a museum-workshop, a knot in the throat, even if it was commonplace. Similarly, the uncharismatic personnel would have no idea how to go about caring for "my" unpublished treasure, which had been represented by a blank page in the novel *Oppiano Licario*. And if I changed my mind before I left Cuba, I could always come back and fulfill my *mea culpa*. If Lezama Lima had been able to wait twenty years to be repatriated, he could wait a few more hours. The immortal dead aren't in any rush. Just the mediocre living. And I wanted to take full advantage of the week Havana would ephemerally unfold for me alone.

3.

The iron effigy of Ché crucified on the Ministry of the Interior was now accompanied by one of Camilo Cienfuegos on the curved façade of the Communications building. Between them, a small crew of shirtless workers pointed up to the bushy eyebrows of the marble Martí at the base of the monolith, which looked so much like mine. Cuba resisted collapse. The older its leaders grew, the more splendid its martyrs.

I crossed the gallery and climbed the esplanade under the sun that always beats down over the island. I paid in strong currency at the gates that guard the most famous monument to global anti-imperialism. And I hid my claustrophobia during the no-less-than-one-hundred-meter elevator ride.

I soon arrived at the top (it was a very modern Otis), panting and with my ears having popped due to the difference in pressure. Then, before looking out through the panels of that supposedly sacred observation deck, I took a few minutes to breathe deeply, so as to avoid the ridiculous scene that would ensue if I fainted among all the Bolivarian tourists with their flash photography, and the tour operators in their military-style *guayaberas*.

I finally looked up. There it was, the precious whore. The lost city that, paradoxically, had changed less in the history books. Urban landscape, stunning and frozen. Stunted with so much retro rhetoric. *Brave New Havana.*

It looked like a flattened labyrinth, a crossword with no clues; a first-generation HavanAtari, perhaps discontinued by the manufacturer. It was the perfect landscape for scattering those papers I so treasured during my four gloomy (and gluttonous) quinquennia of exile. To hurl Lezama Lima as far as I could, so some illustrious or illiterate Habanero could discover him, blocks or kilometers from here. *In Parque Lennon or Parque Lenin,* I thought. Anyway, no one in turn-of-the-century Cuba would recognize the loquacious lyrics of José Lezama Lima, much less his ironic sodomite tics in times not so much of cholera but of collectivization.

What might become of *Summula/never suffused/with morphological exceptions* can be best understood as follows: papers in the wind, tossed to fate, a zeppelin of zeugmas zipping through the claustrophobic atmosphere of my ex-city, an equation that wasn't as much teleological as it was meteorological. It sounds so philosophical and still, it could all end with a fecal performance: imagine, a Cuban poetically wiping his ass with the posthumous prose of *Oppiano Licario*. A light and laughable destiny in the midst of such terrestrial totalitarian ideology. A project I realized was unachievable, after thirty minutes of contemplation, as soon as I noticed that the glass panels at the observation deck were hermetic, just like the total paradise inhabited by the characters invented by José Lezama Lima.

Not even from the highest point in "the capital of all Cubans" could I rid myself of the secret load that had been living with me for twenty years in the form of these stolen originals. The tip of our bitter candy, shaped like the Plaza de la Revolución, had been crowned by a kind of space helmet, while I, on the other hand, was still struggling for air, hours after descending from this urban Turquino with the papers of that fat ogre from Trocadero 162 beginning to reek under my armpit.

4.

Nighttime in Havana has an almost oppressive radiance. Less oppressive if you're by the sea. Agonizing if you're sixty and for the last third of your life haven't once sat on the Malecón's slick concrete redolent of fish.

Alone. It's a privilege to be alone. To be the final witness to an atrocity. A notary, an archivist, a spy. "I don't miss a thing," I tell myself, "I'm not even back on a visit right now—I was never entirely gone." And if his call hadn't been apocryphal (someone's partner told someone else about me, who told him, I later found out), Germán should materialize any time now.

The street vendors sold everything along the roadway. *Maní*, milk caramels, corn nuts, bread with whatever, DVDs with legal licenses to be pirated, planners from the year 2012, brand-name tobacco, talismans guaranteed for one night only, and even glass flowers with little 3-volt light bulbs in them. All of it cheap, no packaging, ready to be tossed out the next morning under the same dim streetlight where it had been purchased. You could get a trio to sing you an off-key bolero, or buy a horrifying photograph of yourself taken with full-on flash (black background like in a studio and me burned into the foremost foreground: a vaudeville Diego, or Devil). And, of course, there was sex for sale in all colors and at all prices, in this or that currency, in dialects ranging from poor to *high-life*.

December had tried to dress itself for winter. And Germán's call to my hotel room hadn't been the joke of some impersonator. Just like the Reaper, Germán arrived on that moonless night right on time, at 10:10. He had a habit of making symmetrical appointments, where the hours and minutes added up to a number that was significant to the people involved (in this case, my twenty years of exile, 10 + 10).

He approached from afar, already smiling, a Germán who wasn't Germanic at all but tropical, with his clueless bastard expression, which twisted into a grimace as he threw himself upon me. We embraced, he cried. He whimpered like a child. Economically, I produced one and only one tear, perhaps at seeing someone I remembered as cynical grow so emotional.

He didn't manage to get ahold of himself for the rest of the night. There was reason for his discomposure beyond our reunion and his certain weaknesses. He st-st-stuttered. He popped pills of different varieties during our conversation. I told him I'd send him a few botanical infusions: *homeopathy for homosexuals*, I teased, but we didn't even smile. I felt sorry for his winner's frustration. Or his liar's megalomania. Germán swore he had exposed his artwork as much as possible, in Cuba and abroad. But it was his enemies' aesthetic jealousy, he said, that kept him from being nominated for National Prizes awarded each year by MINCULT, a veritable piñata for artists who paid with their silent complicity before the unending establishment.

Germán hadn't loved another man after me—I pretended to believe—only choosing to fornicate in bulk with all kinds of races and professionals from the insular proletariat (and with his gallery owners from the European left). He had an obsolete LADA that he never drove himself. He had his own studio, but he painted little and sculpted even less. And he had copious amounts of HIV antibodies in his blood, though not one symptom of AIDS in ten years. "Thanks to P-p-papá Cuba," and he p-p-proclaimed this without a trace of sarcasm, since it was the State that provided him with an antiretroviral cocktail imported from any country that would allow it, given the embargo laws enforced against Cuba by my new country.

As we said goodbye near the little bones around the vandalized monument to the Marines of the USS *Maine*—which was missing its original imperial eagle, but also the pacifist dove promised by Pablo Picasso—Germán extracted his dental prosthesis as if it were a unidentified foreign object: "Look, look at this, Dieg-g-go. Damn," and he held it out to me, crying again without stuttering.

Before he disappeared down Avenida Paseo, into the mist that rolled in from the phallus tower in the Plaza de la Revolución and gathered around the wires and the palm trees, my ex-love-turned-ex-friend-turned-ex-nobody surprised me with a phone number for Nancy, our dear snitch of a neighbor: "Don't w-w-wait if you're going to call her," he said, polite but pressing. "Every day for t-t-twenty years now that w-w-whore has been threatening to kill herself."

5.

She had moved from Buenavista to Pogolotti, from Pogolotti to Puentes Grandes, from Puentes Grandes to San Leopoldo, from San Leopoldo to Luyanó, and from Luyanó to Lawton. "That's how Nancy is," she said, referring to herself in third person: "if she stops moving, she bursts inside like a whizgig." She looked lovely and worn, I thought. "Ay, Dieguito, you know. Nancy changes house because she doesn't want anything to do with Nancy. And you, have you been living out in the real world?"

I told her about my travels through half of America and Europe. Her eyes never lit up. It was as if I were summarizing the plot of some boring travel novel where they never really go anywhere. She hid her lack of enthusiasm with diplomacy. She didn't try to burden me with the apathy of a Cuban with no passport. She smiled and covered her chipped teeth with the same Calvinist candor she displayed back in the mid-eighties. She was an angel trapped in a social system with no heaven (justice is human, too human in Cuba). Nancy was, of course, my Borgesian Beatriz from the debacle and accordingly, from her rooftop terrace, Lawton looked like an evil aleph.

Hillocks, staircases, churches and factories in ruins: a cemetery of antediluvian Saurians. Above the horizon, as if they were afloat in Havana's nightless night, the muted lights flickered down by the bay. The sounds of ship horns reached us with eons of delay. And then there were the chilling whistles of the ghost trains that shimmered over the elevated tracks out in the distance, near the thermoelectric plant in Tallapiedra, with its faint white smoke of a dying pope.

"Nancy would give the rest of her years not to end up back at the mental hospital. She wants to die without red tape, with this very landscape before her eyes, which will only be eaten by the earth," she said, without a hint of drama, like a poised ninety-year-old actress. "I'm tired, Dieguito: everyone is very tired in this country. Victory is exhausting. Pour me a drink and then go. You've made me sad. But before you leave I want to give you something: take that book over there that has been eavesdropping on us . . ."

It was a very humble edition of *A Queen in the Garden*, from the Pinos Nuevos story collection issued by Letras Cubanas in 2009. It had been dedicated to Nancy in the large, awkward handwriting of its author. Incredibly: David Álvarez Paz.

"Nancy hasn't heard a word from him since all the fanfare around his launch at the Feria del Libro de La Cabaña," she warned, before my enthusiasm could burn through my scalp. "I'm sure he's only gotten busier, now that he's winning prizes with his writing: wife, kids, house, car . . . We're not missing a thing, isn't that right?"

Yes, we really weren't missing a thing. No, we really were missing something. *Shut up, Nancy, please,* though I never said it aloud: *I'll pour you a drink and then I'll go. I won't let anyone get to me this time around—not you, not Cuba. I'm free, and I'm sorry for those of you who stayed just so you could enjoy the sheer pleasure of not playing the leading role in your own lives.*

"His number is over there. I'm sure it's the same one. Nothing changes that easily around here. He lives in one of those apartments the Ministry of Culture assigns to famous artists. It's easier to control the livestock when they're all in the same building," Nancy said, and her rotten cackle resounded over the rusted roofs of the neighborhood.

Ah, my Nancy Viterbo of the *madrugadas*, naïve victim and vitriolic victimizer, our Beatriz lost forever between ex-child, ex-whore, ex-snitch, ex–psychiatric patient, ex-suicide, ex-mother who aborted fetuses until there were no more, ex-neighbor from whom I escaped when she had reached, in true Lezamian fashion, the height of her indefinition: The Nancy who would survive until the end of time in third person in spite of Nancy (half David, half Diego).

6.

The seven-digit phone number David Álvarez Paz had scribbled back in 2009 still worked. As I dialed, I decided I would privately give him the UNPUBLISHED WORK from *Oppiano Licario*, since he had been so against my taking it with me twenty years before (he was the only Cuban to whom I had confessed my felony).

His building was a renovated Yugoslavian model from the Comecon period that stood at the intersection of Infanta and Manglar, and was the only mass that rose above the level of the asphalt for blocks. Up in his fourteenth-floor apartment with its 360-degree-plus view, David waited for me wearing an Industriales sweatshirt, beach shorts and slide-on sandals. There was no ceremony. It was as if we had just seen each other the day before (or the day before that, at the most). I didn't feel anything that I wouldn't have felt better, alone with myself, on the mezzanine of my rental in Manhattan.

It was Friday; I would be flying back to the USA that weekend. I had very intentionally left him for last. I feared diagnosing in David, too, the ugliness of all the spaces I knew and the sickness of all the people I couldn't recognize. I feared that I had never loved him, though I had only seen him shirtless once. I feared I was the one who was dead, as I suspected days before when I was disembarking from that Made in Cubana de Aviación state store.

During the week I had meandered like a tourist. I spent one day at Varadero beach (a slimy swill of Berlusconis). Another day I went to see the orchids at Soroa and the Jurassic cliffs in the Viñales Valley. Then, the Habana Vieja, which had been declared a World Heritage site by UNESCO long before I left, French cruises and all. And after watching the sun sink down the bay's tight throat, I browsed the luxury hotels and mini private restaurants in Centro Habana, which were like theater sets swarming with the next New Man tycoons (like those nightmarish Roberto Arlt characters).

David had euphorically invited me, during that first phone call, to come to his Balkan-style apartment, number 14-B. But I preferred the Castillo del Morro, the artisan fairs and even the hill at the University, where in 1971 they had expelled me with honors: homosexual and closet believer in God, contentious verging on counterrevolutionary verging on criminal. "A calamity," said Marta Aguirre, the bellicose head of the Marxist Philosophy department, before they punished her for dialectically pursuing the crotch of a now-famous television broadcaster in Miami (she's still alive, so I can't name her).

David promised he would be waiting for me, as he had been in our cinematographically palindromic goodbye of 1991, with a bottle of Stolichnaya: the elixir that induced the vomiting of truths among *tavariches*. But I had mindlessly squandered the few days that separated me from him, from his boyish voice in my ear. I don't think we had ever spoken on the phone, and David had even given me his cell: "I never have credit, so I'll hang up and call you back on my home line." The half-funny, entirely ridiculous way of placing a call in Cuba.

David spoke of recreating our last Lezama dinner, not imagining that I had already planned to give him the treasure that he had likely forgotten about. But I delayed my appearance, and returned to the funereal remains of the walls and the overhanging balconies on the Arcos building. During the tedious afternoons, I would creep into the UNEAC gardens, where not one sacred cow could have recognized me with how foreign I looked, and where I bought magazines in bulk, and I spotted the president of Cuban Writers who, I heard, had quickly become a higher-up in the Central Committee of the Communist Party.

David lurked as Diego paradoxically fled from him. I escaped to the cupolas at the Instituto Superior de Arte. To the tropical forest filled with squirrels along the Almendares River (they flee the zoo at Calle 26 and subsist as pariahs there). I prowled around the Capitolio, like the comrade farmer I had once been, back when I had just arrived from the province to live my chance at utopia. I went on foot up to the Virgen del Camino to leave a *gladiolo* in dollars and a few pert *céntimos* in exchange for a *please, loving mother of God, don't ever make me come back here again.* No one deserves to die twice in the same Havana.

And, like a billiard ball, I rolled through the Machadato neoclassical columns at the University where, the day before that definitive Friday, when I could already taste the domestic seasoning of David's invitation, I saw Ismael, who without recognizing me continued on his path along the Law School, tall, tall, tall like a pine tree (I'll say it: like a penis), wearing a military uniform that reflected his rank. Apollonian, apocalyptic. His skin was weathered, but clean. His step was firm, the step of a man at peace.

Everything that might be expected of an active military man. His gaze was beautiful, like faith until death.

7.

The Lezama dinner was such a complete success (all of them are, except for the original in *Paradise*, Chapter 7) that it's not even worth recounting. It's not worth recounting anything else. That part is clear from the start, and yet we still insist on conjuring the illusion of an ending.

David, telling me about how he published his first stories in Cuba, after growing bored with the profession he had studied for. David, listing all his school friends who had left the country and never contacted him, like me (his *soul* friend, I corrected him). David, showing me photographs of his two children, Teo, fifteen, and Yoani, thirteen, who since the divorce lived with their mother in another identical building, but in Alamar. David, fortunately, with all his teeth intact, an acceptable belly and bottle-bottom glasses (I had gotten LASIK with the money I earned from my first copyright in exile). David, with his baseball sweatshirt and old-man sandals. David, happy with life, with an offensive ignorance of life beyond the Cuban literary world, which, according to the critics (according to David), had been "revolutionized" by his book, *A Queen in the Garden*. Liter-arid camping: I made a serious attempt to laugh at him.

We smoked. We drank vodka. We cracked jokes about women (just because I don't sleep with them doesn't mean I have any less machismo in my repertoire) and jokes about the presidents, about where they could be found, in the case of Russia (or China, or

Venezuela), the Yankee president, the Cuban one. Though neither of us could say exactly who ours had been since Fidel's first death, in the prehistoric summer of 2006. We listened to music: *Habana Oculta y Habana Abierta*, a sad *timba* that we played on a loop on his laptop. A Dell. Delight, delict, control-alt-del.

We heard the cannon go off at nine. Midnight came. We went out to his balcony. The end of the year was around the corner. Havana shimmered blue, an opaque sapphire. It was gorgeous. *I'll be damned*, I thought: *Why have I only come back now? Why not before? Why hadn't I ever come back?* Havana shimmered like a movie set. A cosmodrome. Another planet. And it was nine-hundred-and-fifty-nine times more wet-cold than in New York. David said, pulling on a jacket: "Brother, you're killing me over here." And I said: "I missed you, you queer. Come give me a kiss on the mouth."

We laughed at my remark like two fools (I had been serious when I said it, but I didn't even believe it myself when I heard it out loud) and then we shook hands with the promise that this time we would write emails and become Facebook friends (UNEAC allowed David to have a peso Internet account in his apartment). I told him not to walk me downstairs. And I left. But I never called the elevator. I found the emergency stairs and, instead of using them, sat down on one of the steps, on the verge of passing out.

Were we really David and Diego? Or had they replaced us with mutant clones? Were we the David and Diego who had fallen in love in this city without knowing it, once or never? Or had it all been a blur, a stupor, a void? Were we going to die without seeing each other's unconcealed dicks and buttock folds? Without tasting each other's ethyl breath? Without exchanging a single truth? And I'm not talking about fucking, understand, but about knowing that today we have a body and tomorrow a cadaver. And I am talking about fucking, understand well, about knowing that today we have a body and tomorrow a cadaver.

Like Fidel.
Like Cuba.
Like the Revolution.

After half an hour I got up. I had a hard-on. I was dizzy, and wanted to vomit. The Davidian dinner weighed in my stomach like a Carthaginian cannonball. Nausea. Of course I never told David about the unpublished works. Maybe I'd use them back in New York to wrap up my McDonald's, or I'd chew them up with soy sauce and Tabasco in a King Size. Maybe I'd roll them into a joint. Ahistoric smoke. *Cannabis cubensis*. Wafts of will, vertigo. Maybe the detectives at the airport would arrest me for trafficking cultural treasures.

My jacket felt soaked. I began to tremble. I grasped at my face. I had been crying and only then did I notice. Without conflict or cause. To cry on instinct as a reflex or self-preservation. Fuck, it was true: someone had to cry. Fever. I walked down the stairs and out the door. It was already daylight there on the crumbling corner of Infanta and Manglar.

I took a dollar taxi. I must have fallen asleep right away next to the driver, nodding off against the seatbelt. The flight attendant was another giggling *mulata* who helped me with my buckle in a flash, right near the zipper of this countryless queer, right at that timeless time to close the doors and clear out of Cuba forever. To clear Cuba out of myself forever—a variation on a terrible outcome. The noise was deafening. How mysterious, how miraculous, how shitty.

By the time I thought about it again the labyrinthine tangle of New York was emerging like an unbelievable relief in the hermetic window next to my seat, number 666; surely there were more Cubans on board without a Cuba (or with a Cuba in third-person singular impersonal), their hearts overflowing onto the wings of this flying piece of junk marked with the blood red, sky blue, and pure white Cubana de Aviación logo.

I wanted to go back to Cuba, dammit.

But dammit, Cuba most certainly did not want me.

AUTHOR BIOGRAPHIES

JORGE ALBERTO AGUIAR DÍAZ (JAAD)

Born in 1966, Havana. Fiction writer, editor, poet, freelance journalist, writing instructor. He is the author of *Adiós a las Almas* (Letras Cubanas, Havana, 2002). Most of his articles and essays are collected on the Miami-based website *Cubanet* (www.cubanet.org/?s=jorge+alberto+aguiar). He runs the blogs *Fogonero emergente* (jorgealbertoaguiar.blogspot.com) and *Cuarto de máquinas/Compasión por Cuba* (jorgealbertoaguiardiaz.blogspot.com). He also served as editor-in-chief of the independent literary and opinion magazine *Cacharro(s)* (revistacacharros.blogspot.com). Some of his interviews of renowned writers, such as Cuban poet Eliseo Diego, have been published by *El Espectador* (Bogotá, Colombia) and *Casa de las Américas* (Havana, Cuba). He teaches writing at the Narrative Techniques Workshop "Salvador Redonet" and the Creative Writing Laboratory "Enrique Labrador Ruiz" in Havana. A Tibetan Buddhist, he temporarily lives in Spain.

JORGE ENRIQUE LAGE

Born in 1979, Havana. Fiction writer, editor, literary critic. He holds a BS in Biochemistry from the University of Havana's School of Biology (2002). He is the editor-in-chief of the Cuban literary magazine *El cuentero* and editor at Caja China publishing house. His fiction publications include *Yo fui un adolescente ladrón de tumbas* (Extramuros, 2004), *Fragmentos encontrados en La Rampa* (Abril, 2004), *Los ojos de fuego verde* (Abril, 2005), *El color de la sangre diluida* (Letras Cubanas, 2007), *Carbono 14: Una novela de culto* (Altazor, Perú, 2010) and *Vultureffect* (Unión, 2011). He was selected for the international anthology of young Hispanic American writers for the website www.literaturas.com. He lives in Havana.

JHORTENSIA ESPINETA

Born in 1976, Camagüey. Fiction writer, poet, editor, art critic, publicist and cultural promoter. She holds a BS in Art Studies from the Escuela Nacional de Arte, Havana (2003). She is the author of a book of short stories entitled *Zona de exorcismo* (Ácana, 2006). She lives in Camagüey, Cuba.

AHMEL ECHEVARRÍA PERÉ

Born in 1974, Havana. Fiction writer, photographer, editor, webmaster of www.vercuba.com and www.centronelio.cult.cu. He holds a BS in Mechanical Engineering from ISPJAE, Havana. His publications include *Inventario* (Unión, 2007), *Esquirlas* (Letras Cubanas, 2006) and *Días de entrenamiento* (FRA, Prague, Czech Republic, 2012). He has been included in several Cuban literature anthologies, such as *Los que cuentan* (Cajachina, 2007), *La ínsula fabulante: El cuento cubano en la revolución 1959-2008* (Letras Cubanas, 2008) and *La fiamma in bocca: Giovanni narratori Cubani* (Voland, 2009). As a columnist he has collaborated with the independent digital magazine *Voces*, *Diario de Cuba*, *The Revolution Evening Post* and the Dialogue Section of Hermanos Saíz Association (www.ahs.cu/secciones-principales/dialogos/dialogos.html). He lives in Havana, Cuba.

LIEN CARRAZANA LAU

Born in 1980, Havana. She holds a BS from the San Alejandro Fine Arts Academy. Her stories have been included in anthologies like *Vida laboral y otros minicuentos* (Caja China, 2006) and in the literary magazine *El cuentero*. Her first book of short stories is *Faithless* (Habitación 69, México DF, 2011). She works on staff at the opinion, literary and news website www.diariodecuba.com. She lives in Madrid, Spain.

POLINA MARTÍNEZ SHVIÉTSOVA

Born in 1976, Havana. Fiction writer, poet, visual arts performer, freelance journalist. She graduated as a Library Specialist (1999). Her poetry collections published in Cuba include *Gotas de fuego* (Unicornio, 2004) and *Tao del azar* (Unicornio, 2005). She is also the author of *Hechos con Metallica* (2008). She is the winner of the National Short-Story Award "La Gaceta de Cuba" (2006) and the Ibero-American Short Story Award "Julio Cortázar" (2008). In 2010 she was a participant in the research panel entitled "Russian literature in Cuban culture." Her essay "Borsch no liga con Ajiaco" appears in *Caviar with rum: Cuba-USSR and the Post-Soviet Experience* (Palgrave Macmillan, NY, 2012). She is a columnist for the international websites *CubaEncuentro*, *Diario De Cuba* and *CubaNet*. She lives in Havana.

MICHEL ENCINOSA FÚ

Born in 1974, Havana. Editor and novelist. He holds a BS in English Literature. He is the author of *Sol negro* (Extramuros, 2001), *Niños de neón* (Letras Cubanas, 2001), *Veredas* (Extramuros, 2006), *Dioses de neón* (Letras Cubanas, 2006), *Dopamina, sans amour* (Abril, 2008), *Enemigo sin voz* (Abril, 2008), *El Cadillac rojo y la gran mentira* (Loynaz, 2008), *Vivir y morir sin ángeles* (Letras Cubanas, 2009) and *Casi la verdad* (Matanzas, 2009). Besides writing social realism, he is also devoted to science fiction and epic fantasy. He has been included in over twenty anthologies from Italy, Spain, Brazil, Argentina, Mexico and the United States of America.

LIA VILLARES

Born in 1984, Havana. Writer, audiovisual editor, musician, blogger. She holds a BS degree in Music Arts Studies, Havana (2002). Most of her writing remains unpublished. She is the webmaster of the blogs *Habanemia* (habanemia.blogspot.com) and *Arroz con punk* (arrozconpunk.blogspot.com).

ERICK J. MOTA

Born in 1975, Havana. He is the author of *Bajo presión* (Gente Nueva, 2008), *Algunos recuerdos que valen la pena* (Abril, 2010), *Havana underguater* (Atom Press, 2010) and *Ojos de cesio radiactivo* (Red Ediciones, S.L., 2012).

RAÚL FLORES

Born in 1977, Havana. He is the author of *El lado oscuro de la luna* (Extramuros, 2000), *El hombre que vendió el mundo* (Letras Cubanas, 2000), *Bronceado de luna* (Extramuros, 2002), *Días de lluvia* (Unicornio, 2003), *Rayo de luz* (Abril, 2003), *La carne luminosa de los gigantes* (Abril, 2007), *Balada de Jeannette* (Loynaz, 2007) and *Paperback writer* (Matanzas, 2010). His texts have been included in literary magazines and anthologies from Spain, the Dominican Republic, Italy, Mexico, Brazil and the USA.

ORLANDO LUIS PARDO LAZO

Born in 1971, Havana. Fiction writer, blogger, photographer, editor, freelance journalist. He holds a BS in Biochemistry (1994), and he worked as a molecular biologist in the Center for Genetic Engineering and Biotechnology of Havana. He has served as an editor for the cultural magazine *Extramuros,* as well as for several independent Cuban digital magazines, including *Cacharro(s)* (revistacacharros.blogspot.com), *The Revolution Evening Post* and *Voces* (vocescubanas.com/voces). He is the webmaster of the blogs *Lunes de Post-Revolución* (orlandoluispardolazo.blogspot.com) and the photoblog *Boring Home Utopics* (vocescubanas.com/boringhomeutopics). His residence is in Havana. He lives temporarily in the United States, giving university lectures about social activism and Cuban civic society using new media. He is the editor of an anthology of Cuban literature by young authors published by www.sampsoniaway.org, based in Pittsburgh.